By EMIL LUDWIG

❦

WILHELM HOHENZOLLERN

BISMARCK: THE TRILOGY OF A FIGHTER

CONSISTING OF THREE PLAYS—

1. KING AND PEOPLE (1862-1864)
2. UNION (1870)
3. DISMISSAL (1890)

NAPOLEON

BISMARCK: THE STORY OF A FIGHTER

GOETHE

JULY '14

SIR EDWARD GREY

Secretary of State for Great Britain, 1914–

JULY '14

By

EMIL LUDWIG

Author of
"Goethe," "Wilhelm Hohenzollern," etc.

Translated from the German by

C. A. MACARTNEY

*" A man need not have been a
Bismarck to prevent this most
idiotic of all wars."*

BALLIN

With 16 Illustrations

NEW YORK : LONDON

G. P. PUTNAM'S SONS

The Knickerbocker Press

1929

JULY '14

Copyright, 1929
by
G. P. Putnam's Sons

Made in the United States of America

TO OUR SONS—IN WARNING

The thanks of the Translator and the Publishers are due to Dr. J. F. Muirhead for reading the translation both in typescript and in proof and for making very many valuable suggestions.

FOREWORD

THE war-guilt belongs to all Europe; researches in every country have proved this. Germany's exclusive guilt or Germany's innocence are fairy-tales for children on both sides of the Rhine. What country wanted the war? Let us put a different question: What circles in every country wanted, facilitated, or began the war? If, instead of a horizontal section through Europe, we take a vertical section through society, we find that the sum of guilt was in the Cabinets, the sum of innocence in the streets of Europe.

In no country had the man at the machine, in the workshop, or at the plough any desire to break the peace, or any interest in doing so. Everywhere the lower classes feared war and fought against it till the eleventh hour. The Cabinets, on the other hand, the War Offices and interested circles that worked with them, the ministers, generals, admirals, war contractors, and journalists, were driven forward by ambition and fear, by incapacity and greed, and drove the masses forward in their turn. The less control a Government had to fear, the heavier is its historical responsibility. For this reason, while exact calculations of relative responsibility are impossible, one can say that Vienna and Petersburg stand first; Berlin and Paris, their seconds, follow them, although at very different intervals; London comes a long way after.

It is not too early to demonstrate this; more especially as I am not describing the economic and political background, but only July 1914. The documents are not insufficient for this purpose; rather, they are overabundant. The origin of the recent war is known to us more exactly than that of any earlier war in history. It is only those who wish to darken European counsel in nationalist interests that still throw the dust of the archives in our eyes. As early as 1921, when I wrote this book and sent it to the printers, four years before my biography of the Kaiser, the whole story could be read plainly from the documents. Nevertheless, I had the type distributed, feeling that the political parties in Germany, still staggering under the effects of the war, could not yet be expected to take a non-party view. Since that date I have gone through the manuscript repeatedly to keep it abreast of the latest research, including the British documents, but I have found little to correct or to add.

This book, like every historical account, is composed of documents and a commentary on those documents. The documents consist of the Blue Books, on which all writers have drawn, supplemented by memoirs and other recognised sources; the conversations between statesmen, generally reported by them to their Governments in the indirect form, have been retranslated into direct speech, the sense, and, where possible, the original wording being kept unaltered. On the other hand, in order to avoid wearisome analysis, I have frequently couched my interpretations in the form of monologues, in which the actors are made to describe their own thoughts and feelings. The distinction between the two methods of presentation has been emphasised for the benefit of readers and critics by the use of different type. All extracts from documents are printed in italics, so that they can be distinguished at once from the author's work and his opinions. I chose this method because certain historians, who are still attempting to prove the wisdom of the responsible German statesmen of 1914, have queried the authenticity of the sources in my earlier political histories, where these did not suit their purposes.

When excerpts from this book appeared in the American Press in 1928, I was abused in Germany

by those sections of the Press that had formerly
incited the country to war, and so are now preaching the "innocence" of Imperial Germany. At the
same time, the *Figaro* of Paris wrote that I "unfortunately formed no exception to those who were
trying to relieve their country of the consequences
of its defeat." By establishing the universality of
the guilt, I was supposed to be attacking the basis
of the Treaty of Versailles. Every man who aims
at super-national justice is subjected to similar
attacks from both sides.

This book is a study of the stupidity of the men
who in 1914 were all-powerful, and of the true
instinct of those who, at that time, were powerless.
It is *international* in outlook, and shows how a
peaceable, industrious, sensible mass, of 500 millions, was hounded by a few dozen incapable leaders, by falsified documents, lying stories of threats,
and chauvinistic catchwords, into a war which was
in no way destined or inevitable. Economic crises,
questions of competition and colonies had, indeed,
complicated the European situation; yet war had
been averted time and again, and three capable
statesmen could once more have achieved what the
great majority desired. It is a lie that one single
people as such wanted war, or wants it to-day.
The methods of modern warfare have made the

idea of a "warlike nation" an illusion; now there
are only the tempters, who look after themselves,
and the tempted, who succumb. Not one of the
ministers and generals who provoked the war fell
at the front. If Europe does not want to be
dragged into another war, every country must pass
laws forbidding any responsible minister to put on
a gas-mask; then they will at once come to terms.

Where history cannot serve as a model, it should
at least be fruitful as a warning. The picture of
July 1914 shows a continent in which the nations
trusted and obeyed their leaders, while those leaders in their turn were responsible to no central
authority. The absence of any control over the
individual Governments had brought about European anarchy. We know that those who drove
Europe into war were themselves driven. This is
precisely where their guilt lies; they let themselves
be driven. Hurry, carelessness, surprise, and
above all, mutual fear, in the first place reduced
these diplomats to impotence, and finally brought
about a war which a sound League of Nations
could have prevented. That it resulted in the first
attempt to set up such an organisation was inevitable and right.

This book demonstrates the peaceable intentions
of the masses of all nations in July 1914. May it

contribute to strengthen the idea of a Court of Arbitration, which is no Utopia, but a growing reality—not a permanently insoluble problem, but the inevitable outcome of recent experience. Since Europe now consists, for practical purposes, of republics only, it can more easily protect itself against catastrophes.

There is only this alternative: either to do it now, or to wait for another war.

June 15, 1929.

CONTENTS

11

ILLUSTRATIONS

13

14   ILLUSTRATIONS

JULY '14

DRAMATIS PERSONÆ OF
THE GREAT TRAGEDY

FRANZ FERDINAND, *Archduke of Austria.*

SOPHIE, *Duchess of Hohenberg.*

RUDOLPH, *Prince Imperial of Austria.*

WILHELM II.

FRANZ JOSEPH.

NICHOLAS II.

ADMIRAL TIRPITZ, *of Prussia.*

ARISTIDE BRIAND, *Premier of France.*

COUNT LEOPOLD BERCHTOLD, *of Vienna.*

COUNT STEPHAN TISZA, *of Hungary.*

COUNT VON BETHMANN HOLLWEG, *of Berlin.*

COUNT OTTO VON BISMARCK.

COUNT VON JAGOW, *of Berlin.*

RT. HON. RICHARD BURDON HALDANE.

RAYMOND POINCARÉ, *Prime Minister of France.*

SIR EDWARD GREY, *Minister of Foreign Affairs in the British Cabinet.*

COUNT SERGIUS DEMITRIEWITSCH SAZONOV, *of Russia.*

COUNT SUCHOMLINOV, *Minister of War for Russia.*

ISVOLSKI, *Member of the Czar's Cabinet.*

HON. HERBERT ASQUITH, *Premier of the British Cabinet.*

RT. HON. DAVID LLOYD GEORGE, *Member of the British Cabinet.*

RT. HON. WINSTON CHURCHILL, *of the British Government.*

PRINCE LICHNOWSKY, *German Ambassador in London.*

JEAN LÉON JAURÈS, *Leader of the Socialist group in the Corps Legislatif.*

JULES CAMBON, *French Ambassador to Berlin.*

SIR EDWARD HENRY GOSCHEN, *British Ambassador to Berlin.*

MAJOR GENERAL COUNT VON MOLTKE, *Chief of Staff of the Prussian Army.*

COUNT VON BELOW, *Member of the Prussian Cabinet.*

BARON KERENSKY, *Member of the Russian Cabinet.*

JULY '14

CHAPTER I

THE MURDER

THE broad terrace burned in the noonday light. At the foot of the steps the carriage waited; the driver on the box, with his three-cornered hat, motionless behind the caparisoned and equally motionless horses. Four lackeys flanked the steps. Three large French windows were thrown wide open to let the June sun into the red salon of the Belvedere Palace, through which the master of the house must pass on his way from his chapel.

Doors in the Palace flew open, there were rustling, stamping, tramping, calls, children's feet, and men's footsteps; now the Archduke himself is standing in the middle doorway, a bulky form in his tight general's uniform. His eyes are oddly veiled; he seems to see little, as a man emerging suddenly from the gloom of a church and the passion of lonely prayer, blinded by sunlight and the world.

A stately woman stands at his side, her arm lightly laid on his. Three pretty children wait for the good-bye kiss. So they stand, framed in the white doorway, a picture of simple happiness and of human destiny, however exalted.

Franz Ferdinand looks down at this moment on Vienna, his future capital. Vague thoughts mingle in his mind: ambitious, sceptical. From the clipped hedges, baroque fountains, pyramids and triangles of living green in front of him, the murmur of the great city mounts to the palace in which he spends his life—waiting. Once more, as he looks, the tall shoulder and steep spire of the old Cathedral rise sheer out of the clustering houses; while to the left, in a blue haze, stretches a graceful, undulating chain of round and pointed summits. He turns and embraces Sophie, who is to follow him shortly on his journey; all preparations have been made. His gloomy features light in a smile. Now the children press forward in their turn; he kisses them half-absently. Fate spares him any presentiment of eternal farewell. Quickly into the carriage, through the Palace gate, past the smiling, stone sphinxes——

*   *

Who is the man now travelling southward? A
massive head is set squarely on robust shoulders.
Not exactly brutal-looking, but neither elegant nor
supple; this man is strangely un-Austrian, and altogether un-Hapsburg.

There is nothing attractive about him, nothing
lovable. Everything is heavy, defiant: forehead,
hair, moustache. The expression is that of a man
who has learnt to be silent and to suffer, who is
masterful and stubborn, who despises mankind
and looks on the world itself simply as iron for
his anvil; a violent and a fearless man. But his
eyes, grey-blue, and with unusually small pupils,
betray at times a softness unconfessed even to himself; they betray sudden abandonment in love, and
fits of melancholy brooding. His piety, too, seems
to be genuine; his ambition, indeed, no less. It is
difficult to imagine this face in merriment; set between will to power and contempt of it, he seems
fatally swayed by both. It is the head of a doomed
man.

He is fifty years of age now, he is feared, he is
powerful; and yet the life which lies behind him has
not been a rich one. The hates and jealousies of
his Imperial cousins filled his youth. When he was
twenty, their Highnesses the Archdukes, who had
nothing to think about except who would be the

most pliable successor, tried to get this tough customer out of the way; they forced him to renounce
his claims to the Crown, as an invalid, a dying man.
Then Otto, who took his place, ruined his health
prematurely by dissipation, while he, Franz Ferdinand, recovered, and, to the anger of the Imperial
House, became heir presumptive once more, after
all. How they crave for power! How ambitious
and cold they are; and if they cannot overcome
Death, how they try at least to manage him, for a
while!

This Hapsburg had a strain of imagination in
him. The flirtations with which idle princes seek
to embellish their empty lives, the thirst for fresh
vitality which drives this decadent family to the
streets and farms, the current archducal fashion of
collecting love-affairs like dogs or walking-sticks,
seem alien to this man with the square-cut head; he
dreams of a love-match and is resolved not to let
his conception of happiness be distorted by his own
ambition. He picks out a countess; she shall be
his wife, the mother of his children.

Just fourteen years ago he did battle for his
Sophie with the old Emperor. The Emperor said
"no." His own son, Rudolph, had killed himself
for a woman whom his position made it impossible
for him ever to marry—and now was a mere

nephew, whom he detested, to force on him, not
only the succession, but a woman who was not
even of the first nobility; to adulterate with base
blood the legitimate line of the Emperors? But
the nephew defied him; obstinate and resentful,
standing before the old man, he stuck to his resolve,
well aware that they could not get rid of him a
second time.

He had his way and got his bride; but two days
before the wedding, he stood in the little Council
Chamber of the Hofburg and solemnly, before
Emperor and Empire, renounced in advance the
Hapsburg succession for any child whom he should
beget of the Bohemian Countess. A tragic moment
for a man whom piety, loneliness, and perhaps
sentiment too, impelled to marriage; to have now
to deprive the fruits of that marriage, ere yet be-
gotten, of their birthright.

It was inevitable that every year of happy wed-
lock should strengthen his longing to find at last
some indirect means of legitimising his dear mate,
whose children loved him so well and were so good
to look upon. So he contrived to have her created
a duchess, and he tried, with the Princes, his peers,
to remove a prejudice which, in another form,
still surrounded him in every direction. After
long years he enjoyed the triumph of seeing his

wife received by the German Empress herself.
Wilhelm II, the mighty ally on whose consent
Franz Ferdinand's political plans depended, had
always been amiable to Sophie; and though the
friendship between the two men, who were much
of an age, had other foundations deeper than this,
it could never have endured had the Kaiser treated
the Duchess with any lack of courtesy. The Archduke had double reason to be grateful to the
German Kaiser; for Franz Joseph, stiff and
unyielding, clung rigidly to his ceremonial in
Vienna, and at Court made his niece walk behind
the least important of the ladies of the blood
royal.

All the while the Archduke, passionate and defiant, had no keener ambition than to make his
wife Empress, his children heirs to the succession.
The old gentleman had kept him waiting long
enough; but now he was over eighty.

For that reason this day and the next were great
days for him. His wife was to follow him to Bos-
nia, and, after inspecting the XVth and XVIth
Corps, he was going to take her to Sarajevo. There
Sophie was to make her first appearance in state,
as wife of the future Emperor, not in Berlin or
Bucharest, but on the soil of the Monarchy itself.
It was a surprise which he himself had planned,

and only yesterday he had sought assurance that the secret had been kept from his enemies in Vienna.

Franz Ferdinand's thoughts rove restlessly between his own future and his country's. So long as he thinks of Kaiser Wilhelm, he holds to the strictly monarchical basis of his ideas, and he applauds in his powerful friend a conception of royalty which in his own marriage he has not upheld. The Kaiser's idea of sport appeals to him, too. They both look at it in the same way. Unlike Franz Joseph, who would spend days in stalking a single elusive chamois, these two enjoy *battues,* and at the end of the day they love to inspect the long file of corpses, as if they were soldiers on parade.

Furthermore, each holds the other, and rightly, to be a friend of peace. When once a gipsy woman prophesied to the Archduke that he would let loose a great war, he laughed at her. The victor's laurels meant nothing to him. His ambition was once more to shore up his crumbling Empire from within; and for this he had his ideas. His plan was to take Transylvania away from the Hungarians, whom he hated, to attach Roumania to the Monarchy in one form or another, to fulfill the old wish of the Czechs by having himself crowned in Prague as well as Budapest, to transform Dualism into Trialism, or, if necessary, to reconstruct the whole Empire as a federal State of five units.

For this purpose it was necessary to protect the Serbs against the Bulgars without and the Magyars within; to save the loyal Croats from the Hungarian spies, and cautiously drive his wedge between Serb and Croat by making the Slavs within the Monarchy too contented to wish to leave it. Franz Ferdinand was a friend of the Slavs, if not of the Serbs; and now, in travelling towards their frontier, he might fairly hope to find welcoming faces for himself and his wife.

*   *

The low houses of Sarajevo gleam white; the flat roofs reflect the blue of the sky, and bright in the noonday are the gala skirts and jackets of the Bosnians, who have flocked into the city from far and wide to see the foreign Prince who is soon to be called father of their land. All is noise and movement, for to-day is a double feast: the Bosnians welcome the heir of Austria's crown; the Serbs among them celebrate the day on which, five centuries ago, their forefathers were crushed on the Field of Blackbirds—a nation which in song and legend celebrates its greatest defeat as a fearful warning, ever fresh.

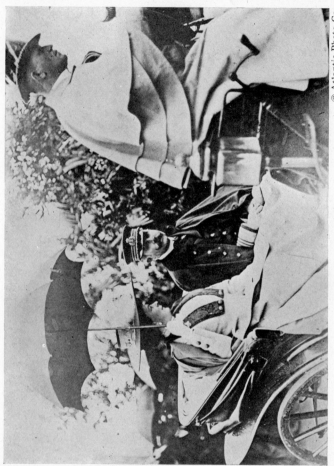

© Atlantic Photo Co.

FRANZ FERDINAND
Archduke of Austria, together with the Duchess

This year, however, for the first time, it has become a day of resurrection, for now at last they have beaten the Turks and the Bulgars. But those hundreds of thousands whom Austria forces to call themselves her subjects, since six years ago Aehrenthal stole the two occupied provinces, Bosnia and Herzegovina—flesh of their flesh—these have a double grudge to-day, because this foreign Crown Prince is to force his presence on them in sign of mastery, and has brought with him a wife, who is not recognised as a real wife in Vienna. This is the story, as these peasants and townsmen have heard it from agents and agitators.

Then, too, what the priests say, violent and confusing, stirs to-day in the excited hearts of this people of three religions, as they jostle one another in the crowded streets of their capital. The Croats pray and confess in Roman style; while the Serbs are only orthodox. For decades it has been a struggle whether race or religion were to prove the stronger bond. Their faith draws the Croats to Western Europe, and so to Austria; blood ties them to their Serbian brothers. "To-day we will ask him"—so the gaily-dressed Croats are thinking —"to-day, when he has drunk a few glasses of our sweet, heavy wine at the feast in the Konak. Is Budapest to go on treating us like a pack of thieves, or will not Vienna remember our Jellatchitch, who laid his bloody sword on the altar of St. Stephen and saved Austria from the rebel Magyars?"

"What a lot of strangers there are in the town to-day," thinks the Chief of Police, a Hungarian civil servant, as he drives through the streets; but he says nothing. As the visit is to be *"purely military,"* precautionary measures have been left to the troops; the civil police force, 150 men strong, has only its normal duty of preserving public order. "How few soldiers there are about," thinks the Chief of Police; and again says nothing. What is the Minister in Vienna thinking about, to take no precautions? But the Governor, too, has given no special orders. He could not, he said, very well line the streets with troops; for the Archduke is coming with his wife, and that would make it an entry in state of the future Emperor.

Four cars pass swiftly through the suburbs. From afar come shouts of *Zivio;* joyous shouts, not fierce. Now they are turning on to the Quay; in the first car the Government Commissary and the Burgomaster, in the second the Archduke and his wife; facing them Potiorek, Governor of Bosnia and Herzegovina, and beside the chauffeur a certain Count Harrach, of the motor corps, to whom the car belongs. In the third and fourth cars are the suite. Then the crowd grows denser, the shouts become louder; on the farthest frontier of his Empire, in the disputed storm-centre, the Archduke feels himself welcomed; and at his side he sees his wife—sees her acknowledge the cheers like an Empress. The moment intoxicates him a little; for her sake, and because he has achieved fulfilment of the desire of years. They draw near the City Hall.

Suddenly, at half-past ten, a crack like a rifle-shot is heard on the right of the car, a small object falls on the hood behind the couple and rebounds; only when the next car has passed does the bomb explode, with a roar like a cannon.

All the cars stop. Two officers of the suite are wounded. The Archduke sends help. The Colonel, whose injuries are grave, is taken to the hospital. Meanwhile the thrower of the bomb has run away over the Miljacka Bridge. He is pursued, caught on the far bank. He is an Austrian Serb, a young compositor, Cabrinovitch by name. Ten minutes later the cars drive on.

At the City Hall the councillors are waiting to receive their guest, who bursts out, pale and furious, *"So you welcome your guests here with bombs?"* No one answers. The horrified burgo-master makes his speech to uneasy listeners. When the Archduke prepares to answer him, he perceives that his voice is trembling, and forces it to be firm. His wife receives the wives of the local Society leaders. Do not he and she both feel how absurdly prosaic this scene really is, on which they had based such high hopes? Was it for this that they had escaped death by inches—to stand in this unpretentious building, laboriously decked out to look festal with a few carpets, and hear two stupid speeches?

They step forward. The crowd cheers loudly. Count Harrach asks the Governor in astonishment, *"Has not your Excellency arranged for a military guard to protect His Imperial Highness?"*

"Do you think Sarajevo is full of assassins, Count Harrach?" retorts the Governor sarcastically.

Pale and uneasy, the Archduke alters the programme. He proposes to go alone to the hospital to ask after the wounded officer, while his wife goes on to the Konak, where luncheon awaits them. She, however, insists on accompanying him; and he silently yields. As a precaution they decide to take a different route. Young Count Harrach proposes, in default of better protection, to stand on the left foot-board beside the Archduke. Franz Ferdinand says to him sharply:

"Don't make a fool of yourself."

The four cars drive off, exactly as before, only faster.

The crowd is denser and more excited; they shout *Zivio,* but it is only when an old woman cries (in Czech) *Nazdar* that Sophie's pale lips smile. At the entrance to the Franz Joseph Strasse, which had lain on the original route, the crowd, still uncontrolled by police, had left a lane for their passage.

"By a fatal error" the first car turns the corner into the street. Misled by this, the second chauffeur follows. Governor Potiorek, author of the sarcasm, the man on whom the whole responsibility rests, calls to him that there has been a mistake and that he is to drive straight on along the quay. Thus the car comes close up to the right-hand pavement, the chauffeur slowing down.

Suddenly two shots ring out from the right-hand side of the street, not ten feet away. Apparently no one is hurt. The Governor, perceiving too late that Sarajevo *is* full of assassins, leaps up and tells the chauffeur to turn back and make for another bridge. At this moment the Duchess sinks upon her husband's breast. The Governor hears a few murmured words pass between the two. Now, and not till now, does he realise that something may have happened.

But the Archduke sits upright. The suite come

running up. No one yet perceives that he has been hit; in his wife's case, too, they suspect no more than a faint. Then blood gushes from his mouth, he sinks crookedly down. They open his uniform. Blood spurts from the great artery on the right side of the neck, over his green uniform and over the cushions of the car.

The Duchess, who has been leaning against him as though she had turned to him for protection, is unconscious, but no wound is visible. They drive to the Government buildings. The two are carried up to a room next to that in which the champagne bottles are cooling. Doctors find a bullet wound in her abdomen, while the Archduke is bleeding to death from the severed artery. A Franciscan monk gives them both absolution; then arrives the Archbishop who had warned him. A quarter of an hour later, death has come to the Archduke Franz Ferdinand of Austria-Este, heir apparent to the Hapsburg Monarchy. A few minutes before him died Sophie, Countess Chotek, Duchess of Hohenberg, the only human being in whom this misanthrope trusted—and the very one rejected by the rest of their world. His last words may have been for her; hers for him; no one overheard them. There is no one to mourn for him. Only the children weep in the Belvedere Palace.

Meanwhile the crowd has seized the murderer. He had hurriedly swallowed cyanide, but vomited it up again. He is a High School student, a Serb by race, an Austrian subject. His name is doubly symbolical, Gabriel Princip—"Bringer of tidings." To what end these tidings? And tidings of what principle?

*   *

Three hours later, in Kiel Bay, a motor-launch drew near the *Hohenzollern,* the Imperial yacht. The Kaiser Wilhelm, dressed as an admiral, stood on deck under the awning, umpiring the race. By turning his eyes a little eastward he could see a few black ships silhouetted against the sun. They were flying the Union Jack. Churchill himself, First Lord of the Admiralty, had wanted to come in person with these English ships, the first which had appeared at the Kiel Week for nineteen years; but Tirpitz had refused *"to sit at the same table with that adventurer."* The Kaiser did not miss the Englishman; he had already had more than enough, on the previous evening, of his Ambassador to England's protestations of England's love of peace. He had, however, been expecting Briand. He would have liked a talk with that citizen of Paris, and had sent him an invitation through the Prince of Monaco. But Briand had not come. Why?

Caution, mistrust between the three countries. The little Italian, too, was growing ever more reserved. Was there anyone left to trust in, except the Old Gentleman in Vienna?

Now the launch has reached the side of the ship. Those on the launch beckon to those on deck. The Emperor waves them away; he will not be bothered. But the officer in the launch insists, holds up a telegram, puts it in a cigarette-case significantly, and throws it on board the yacht. The orderly picks it up, stands at attention before His Majesty. The Kaiser reads the news from Sarajevo. He bites his lips, then says: *"Now I shall have to begin all over again."* The races are put off, the Kiel Week is at an end. The Kaiser paces the deck. His thoughts may very well have been as follows:

"Regicides! I always loathed those Serbian swine! Irreligious through and through! What a scoundrel that Peter looked when I saw him! It was murder put him on the throne, and it's no good pretending it was the Grace of God. Not to us, anyway. . . . So little Karl comes next in the line. Nothing in him but a strict legitimist—so politeness won't go far with him. One could do any-

thing with Franz by sending that fat old Chotek
an invitation to dinner. I shall have to go to
Vienna. But how will they be buried? She can't
possibly be laid in the Imperial vault. The Old
Gentleman couldn't stand the Archduke, anyway.
He was a good chap, really. Five thousand stags,
when one's well under fifty—a pretty good record
that. Only no feeling at all for higher things.
Music and poetry, humanity's supreme achieve-
ments, merely bored and puzzled him. Collected old furniture—that's all. No gift for lan-
guages, either—those queer fits of silence. . . .
Will this make the Vienna people take any special
steps? Not a bit of it, those heroes will funk it
again. . . . Telegram!" And he writes: *"I have
received with deepest distress the tidings of the
ruthless murder . . ."*

*   *

"How is it possible?" cries Europe. "Woe to
those responsible! They shall answer for it, to
their cost!"

Strange things are done, stranger things left
undone. The investigations last only a few days,
and are conducted with an unwonted secrecy. Is
someone being screened? What is being done to
Potiorek, the Governor, who pledged his word that

all was safe, kept up an attitude of injured innocence even after the first explosion, ordered no
troops up to defend his master between the two attempts, and then, at the critical point, where fast
driving was impossible, took the wrong road, corrected it, drove back again, and never so much as
noticed that his master and mistress had been
quietly bleeding to death? No defence was possible for him, so all the more readily they left him
unmolested.

What has the head of the Administration to say?
Ritter von Bilinski, who surely knew more than the
Archduke would have cared for. And is there to be
no inquiry into the conduct of the Chief of Police,
whose men let *"six or seven"* persons well known to
them stand about the street with bombs and re-
volvers, both before and after the first bomb? Not
one policeman has been arrested. Are higher
powers behind them?

Afterwards, the Governor of Agram confided
to his friends—not in Court, so the statement is
hard to check—that at the beginning of June he
had received an anonymous warning from Belgrade, giving the names of the conspirators. He
had passed the letter on to the Government of
Croatia, which gave it to the Hungarian Govern-

ment. But no answer came from Budapest to
Agram, and consequently it was nobody's job to
watch for the murderers' arrival when they crossed
the frontier punctually as announced. Meanwhile
Dr. Gagliardi, an Agram lawyer, had come to the
police with the same warning. The Hungarian
Government has nothing to say on this point either.

But though the Austrians and Hungarians are
being treated, or rather, are treating one another,
with such brotherly consideration, they are free to
turn their wrath and vengeance against the Serbs,
who are obviously guilty, the whole nation of them,
of this murder. If only it could be traced to Belgrade! That is what Vienna hopes. If only a
Serbian Minister, at least, could be compromised!
Then, at last, one could let fly at them! "Find out
everything possible," the Ballplatz calls after Herr
von Wiesner, as he hurries to the scene of the
crime to study the documents. Find out something to be used against the Serbian Government,
Herr Sektionsrat!

Von Wiesner searches, noses out what he can;
but, as an honourable man, the following is all he
can telegraph to Vienna after a fortnight. Firstly: *"The material covering the period before the
assassination gives no grounds for supposing prop-*

*aganda fostered by Serbian Government. Scanty
but sufficient material to effect that this movement
nourished from Serbia through associations, Serbian
Government tolerating.*" Secondly: "*No proofs
of complicity of Serbian Government in organisation or preparation of crime or supply of arms—
In fact, reason to suppose this out of the question.*"
Thirdly: "*Irrefutable and impartial proof that
origin of bombs Serb Army stocks, but no grounds
to suppose them taken from stores* ad hoc, *as they
may come from war supplies of comitadjis. Other
investigations after crime throw light on organisation of the propaganda through Narodna
Obrana. Valuable material here which can be
used, but has not yet been sifted; urgent inquiries
are in progress.*" The report names as the sole
persons compromised, with any certainty: Serbian
frontier and customs officials, one Serbian major,
and a Bosnian railway official.

No political consequences then need be feared.
Charges ought to be brought against Croats and
Hungarians, but none can be brought against any
Serb of consequence.

Meanwhile the murderers have been examined.
One of them, Cabrinovitch, son of an Austrian
subject in Sarajevo, had taken the lead, trained
and instructed his younger companions, and

smuggled the weapons over the frontier. They, with several others, concocted a plot in Belgrade against the Archduke's life.

Was not the day one of time's revenges? The entry in state fell on the date on which their forefathers had once been crushed by the Turks; but on that date, too, young Milos Obilitch had murdered the conqueror Murad and become a national hero, so that the name of Milos lives on to-day in song and legend. To become a second Milos— though one perish for it!

Princip, four years at the High School in Belgrade, then connected with the patriotic societies, and thus imbued with the Greater Serbian dream, a young man with dark, resolute eyes, declares in Court: *"I held the Archduke to be our mortal enemy; he wanted to prevent the unification of all the Southern Slavs!"* Therefore he had resolved to kill him, and himself afterwards, so as to keep the secret safe. He exculpates all the other prisoners, refuses to give names, in order to shield the rest, has never made capital out of his ideas; of his own free will he determined to sacrifice his life to the highest ambition of his people. His attitude is manly, simple, that of a fanatical idealist, like many anarchists. There is nothing against him except this crime, which he conceived to be the only means to achieve his end. He is condemned to twenty years' imprisonment. After three years of continuous darkness, he succumbs. Three others are executed.

Wiesner's report, however, is kept from the public, kept even from Austria's allies; the Serbian Government must remain guilty.

* *

Black and stormy clouds gather over the land; torches cast a weird light on the sodden road, in front of the two tall, black hearses in which the coffins of the murdered pair jolt towards the Danube. They are travelling to Artstetten, to the vault which the Archduke himself had built. "Rather with Sophie on our estate than without her in the Capuchins' vault"—so Franz Ferdinand had thought once, he who loved this woman more than the trappings of power.

Suddenly a fearful storm breaks; the horses are unharnessed, and after a time the coffins are carried back into the little waiting-room of Pöchlarn station. Once again they stand cold and silent beside the boxes and trunks, as though doomed never to find the rest they sought. Later, when they reach the Danube, heavy waves, lashed by rain, overflow the banks as the coffins are borne at last, on the black ferry-boat, over the river.

CHAPTER II

THE WAR COUNTS

RECLINING at ease in their baroque arm-chairs, slender legs in soft, light-grey trousers, comfortably crossed—so two middle-aged counts are sitting in the golden and red chancellery of the Viennese Foreign Ministry. A scent of limes from the Volksgarten is wafted through the tall, open windows. Still in Vienna at the beginning of July? Have they affairs of State to transact? Yes, they are discussing whether one can wear tussore or only grey. Court mourning in the summer is always a nuisance, and the black band on a tussore sleeve would really look too much like the national colours. As they talk in low, reflective tones, each is trying to impart a tone of sadness to his trivial remarks, in the hope that the other will be impressed; as a matter of fact, however, both are pleasantly excited by the event at Sarajevo.

The names of these Imperial and Royal cava-

liers? They are long, and history will know them
simply as Berchtold and Forgátch. Since we,
however, are eavesdropping at a supreme psychological moment, historical accuracy compels us to
introduce them formally. Leopold, Count Berchtold, von und zu Ungarschitz, Fratting, and Pul-
litz, Minister of the Imperial and Royal House-
hold and of the Foreign Affairs of the United
Kingdoms and Provinces: face oval, chin rather
pointed, nose fine, eyes tired, prematurely bald,
moustache clipped short above a sensual, weak
mouth, cynical and blasé, one of the most elegant
gentlemen of Vienna, persuasive when he wishes
to be, agreeable when he has to be, superficial in
thought, careless in action, uncertain in decision,
with the expression of a pampered worldling and
sportsman, who prefers breeding horses for the
race-course or the army to riding them; in every
way a man who enjoys guiding and surveying life
from the grand-stand, setting stallion and general,
soldier and trotting-horse, in motion according to
his own ideas.

The other looks more of a man; a typical Cap-
tain of Hussars, dark, a Magyar. Another fine
name: Count Forgátch von Ghymes and Gács, till
recently Austro-Hungarian Minister in Belgrade,
where, at the Friedjung trial, he was taken in by

LEOPOLD, COUNT VON BERCHTOLD
Secretary of State in the Cabinet of the Emperor Francis Joseph

forged documents with which Austria was attacking her Croat subjects; thus a sufficiently old hand in the diplomatic service to have now become Under-Secretary to his bosom friend, and at the same time secret Envoy Extraordinary of Hungary to Count Berchtold. He it is who, during the past three years, has constantly stimulated the quickly flagging energies of the Minister with "Something must be done!"

Last year, between ourselves, Berchtold made a proper fool of himself. The Treaty of Bucharest, a nasty jar, must be relegated to oblivion: that is the ambitious Count's guiding thought. That treaty increased the territory and the power of three Balkan States, particularly of Serbia. The Foreign Office made itself ridiculous in the eyes of the Army, which mobilised twice to no purpose; and if office and reputation are not both to go, it absolutely must be upset. The year before, Bulgaria had promised Serbia military assistance, even against ourselves, although we supported Bulgarian liberty everywhere. Then Berlin got restive, and supported Roumania and Greece, the two non-Slavonic States, against us. Two bad defeats for the Minister!

Now is the moment for revenge! No need for a battle-cry, the golden old word "prestige" is enough. Anyway, are not all the backers of the Jewish press practically anti-Serb democrats? And even though the Archduke was detested by all his future subjects, except perhaps in the Tyrol, where the Papal Benediction had made him popular, yet it will be easy to raise the cry of an offended nation: Austria's prestige is in danger from the murderous Serbs! So the Ballplatz gets its backing, Isvolski foams at the mouth, San Giuliano whistles gently through his teeth, and the fellows in Berlin, who are always abusing us for slackness, open their mouths in wonder!

Every day the inner dangers grow; in every hole and corner one finds despondency, hatred, passion, obstruction, a babel of tongues, government officials transacting instead of acting, faint-hearted Parliamentarians. Behind the thin layer of intelligence in the great modern towns stands an enormous mass of heavy-witted peasants, some of whom can neither read nor write, cling to their acres, still hunt the bear in Transylvania, and provide workers for the factories in North Bohemia. Only a forcible gesture from the Monarchy will teach Kramarž that it is still alive—but to mobilise a third time and *then* not go for the enemy? Then the guns will go off at home, and the fat will be in the fire! No more diplomatic victories, then! Each fresh concession makes these Serbian bandits only more insolent than ever. Either we must buy their pigs or prepare for war. Ever since Bucharest it's been impossible to breath in Bosnia, which is almost half Serbian. Bilinski, the Pole, seems to be stirring up trouble, too. Keep the Roumanians neutral at least, bring Ferdinand over gently, if Berlin——

Berlin! When will such an opportunity come again? Assassination of a Royal personage has an automatic effect on Wilhelm: punitive expedition on the Chinese pattern, conspiracy against the Imperial House, mailed fist, shining armour. Fulldress uniform, then; autograph letter from the Old Gentleman. But whom shall we send to Berlin? Perhaps little Hoyos; they like him there, and he will see that old Szögyény doesn't put his foot in it. But what shall we say to the Old Gentleman? After all, it's done in his name, and if something goes off suddenly, he may be frightened to death; in that case little Hoyos would be on the mat, and it would be all up with us. What shall we ask Berlin to give us? A general understanding in the Nibelungen style? Will they be good for that? Anything is possible there. With a promise of that sort in our pockets, we could start things off straight away. Hötzendorf has been as keen as mustard for five years, and Krobatin for three. *"Serbia,"* he

said yesterday, *"can be finished off in four weeks."*
Quickly, before Russia knows what's happening to
her beloved child! . . . Everyone is mightily relieved that Wilhelm is not coming to the funeral;
otherwise the two Imperial Majesties would have
been embracing again with tears of peace. All are
full of the joy of battle; some even think it will
be possible to localise the conflict.

Danger? Russia swallowed her medicine all right
five years ago, when Aehrenthal took the two provinces. Big Russia wants to get to the warm, open
sea, and has exactly the same right to do so as little
Serbia. Therefore, it is our historical mission to stop
them both. If they still go on wanting, how is one
to keep the peace? If the crash comes soon, *tant
mieux pour nous!* That thief and murderer Pashitch is not really an enemy worth sacrificing one's
summer holiday to destroy. But the great struggle
against Russia, the supreme end, before which even
Aehrenthal stopped short! In two years Russia will
have her railways finished. Who is going to promise that we shall be here in two years? Quick! Let's
begin on the memorandum for our Imperial master!

A little later, Count Berchtold wrote to his Ambassador in Rome that exploring all the possibilities
of the next few weeks would be like taking a walk
through the Labyrinth. *"At present I have the im-*

*pression that I have been selected by Providence
to become one of those Ministers—from Cardinal
Fleury to Lambsdorff—who wished to make a
policy of peace and were forced into one of war. I
hope I shall have better success than the last man
who took this course."*

*   *

Count Tisza is against it.

The most capable man in the country, and also
the most powerful, is against the Serbian war
planned by the two other Counts. Will he impose
his veto and stop it? Will Reason find a refuge in
the breast of this sinewy Hungarian? Shall we find
here a serious European, alive to his fearful responsibility, and determined to prevent war under
any circumstances—*any* war whatever?

He does not look like a pacifist. The best fencer
and speaker for leagues around, courageous, indomitable, cloaking an iron will under a gentle
manner, old-fashioned in his oligarchical view of
life, disloyal towards the other half of the Empire,
fundamentally hostile to anything outside Hungary; but within these limitations, a statesman with
a knowledge of mankind, always alert, never weary,
always the first in any company. Withal, in his
old-fashioned clothes, he looks like a schoolmaster.

Enormous glasses, like owl's eyes, shield his searching glances from the searching glances of others, as
though this master of the rapier wore a fencing-
mask permanently over his face. With his long
silences, his quick, epigrammatical talk, combining
spiritual with physical activity, he has something
of the old-fashioned hero of romance and makes an
impression on women.

Count Stephan Tisza's feelings, when the wire
brought him the news of the murder of Franz
Ferdinand, that enemy of Hungry, were mixed.
No more danger now of the universal suffrage with
which the Archduke had hoped to break the supre-
macy of the Magyars in Hungary, over the Germans, Roumanians, Croats, and Slovaks; *"Trialism,"* the idea of an independent Yugo-Slavia—a
single shot had brought the whole structure down in
ruins. Could we expect Count Tisza to be very
unhappy in that first quarter of an hour?

In the second quarter of an hour the politician
in him grew reflective. Will not Berchtold's ambition seize this marvellous opportunity of at last
launching a war against Serbia after so many
false starts? Will Forgátch let himself be talked
over by his friends in Vienna? For Tisza the
supreme danger is a victory over Serbia; this would
increase the numbers of Slavs in the monarchy by

millions, and so upset the sacred principle of equilibrium between Hungary and Austria to the advantage of the latter. Moreover, it would cause unrest among the Croats and Roumanians in Hungary, and thus endanger Tisza's entire policy,
which he had based on the subjection of all to the
Magyars.

In Vienna Tisza soon learns that Berchtold is
really proposing to strike. The urgent step now is
to put pressure on the Old Gentleman; accordingly, Tisza writes to his Emperor that: *"I cannot
identify myself with Count Berchtold's intention
of making the crime in Sarajevo an occasion for
settling accounts with Serbia. I have made no
secret from Count Berchtold that I should look
on this as a fatal error, and should in no case agree
to share the responsibility for it. In the first place,
we have as yet no sufficient grounds for putting
the responsibility on Serbia, or for provoking a war
with that State in the face of possible satisfactory
explanations from the Serbian Government. We
should have the worst locus standi imaginable; we
should be exposed before the whole world as the
peace-breakers, and should be starting a great
war under the most unfavourable circumstances.
Secondly, I consider the present moment, when we
have practically lost Roumania, and when Bul-*

*garia, the only State on which we can reckon, is
completely exhausted, to be a most unpropitious
one in every way. In the present Balkan situation,
there can be no difficulty whatever in finding a
suitable* casus belli *whenever it is needed."*

And he urgently recommends breaking down
Germany's hostility to Bulgaria, and taking advantage of the German Kaiser's presence *"to make
use of the recent outrages to destroy this august
personage's prejudiced pro-Serbian attitude, and
to induce him to give active support to our Balkan
policy."*

A little masterpiece, this letter, a piece of rapier-
play in which lunge and parry follow one another
like lightning. An unmistakable threat of resignation is combined with a threat that Hungary's dictator will impose Hungary's veto. It is plain that
Tisza has the decision in his hands. Will he stand
fast?

*   *

In his villa in Ischl, whither he has returned with
all speed after the funeral ceremony, the old Emperor sits in his shooting-coat over the letter which
Berchtold, his Foreign Minister, has laid before
him. If long experience could make a statesman,
Franz Joseph in his old age ought to be cleverer
than in his youth. The fact that, having lost all

his wars, he wants no more of them, does not mean
that he is a convinced pacifist; and in spite of the
Spanish isolation with which this last Emperor in
history "hedges his divinity," he has an ear for the
voice of his subjects; he feels and considers the
wishes of the officers and officials, German and
Hungarian, who are the last props of his artificial
throne. His heart is in nowise moved by his nephew's death; he never liked the Archduke, and his
impossible marriage had intensified dislike into
such detestation that he saw in the news of the
double murder nothing but the judgment of God,
and said at once to his adjutant: *"The Almighty
will not be defied."* Three days after these cruel
words, he is considering the prospects for his deer-
stalking, which, after all he has lost, remains for
him the last delight in life. He cares little who
shall reign after him; probably he realises that
this Empire, which contains so many centrifugal
forces, is held together now only by a universal
respect, amounting to reverence, for his advanced
age; a certain dignity and majesty make intimacy
impossible with this born Emperor, even more
than with the Tsar of All the Russias.

Nevertheless, one must not grow weary; one
must see what is stirring inside the Empire, and,
if necessary, try to use the outer danger to avert

the inner. A few days ago he said to the German Ambassador, who came to excuse the Kaiser Wilhelm's absence: *"I see a very dark future . . . I do not know whether we can afford to look on quietly any longer, and I hope that your Kaiser also realises the danger to the Monarchy caused by the neighbourhood of Serbia. What is particularly disquieting to me is the Russian practice-mobilisation which is planned for the autumn, precisely the time when we are changing the contingents of recruits. . . . With such sensible men as Venizelos and Streit we shall certainly go farther along this right road. Although I certainly do not think much of King Ferdinand, yet Bulgaria is undoubtedly a great country and capable of important development. . Bulgaria is, with the possible exception of Greece, the only Balkan State which has no interests hostile to those of Austria. I therefore consider it proper to cultivate good relations with that country. . . . I know that your Kaiser has complete confidence in King Carol; I have not. . . . If only we could detach England altogether from her friends, France and Russia."*

Here, in a few bars, the whole gamut is sounded. The tone is neither rich nor expressive, but the chords are true enough.

Now, as he sits before the memorandum which

contains the plans against Serbia, memory can
really recall nothing that is good. The past cannot but incline him towards the snares which Berchtold spreads, and before them Tisza's warnings
soon die away. Years ago, the last Obrenovitch
had frustrated his kindly intentions, that same
Alexander who first behaved like a monster to his
father, Milan, and then placed himself beyond the
pale by that marriage with his Draga. Murder of
such creatures could hardly be described as regicide.

Then came Peter—more suspect still; for if
Alexander was murdered, Peter has gained his
throne through the murder. And yet the old Emperor decided to receive him. Everything was ready
in Budapest, three years ago—train, carriages,
banquet all arranged, and then the King of Serbia suddenly took fright and put it off. That is another grudge which a Hapsburg can never forget
against him; still less the two mobilisations which
Peter forced on him. And now one of these Serbs
shoots a Hapsburg in an Austrian street, and sends
him unshriven to his doom! No, Berchtold is right
—and he signs the memorandum written out for
him, containing the following words to the Kaiser
Wilhelm:

*"The assassination of my poor nephew is the
direct result of the agitation carried on by the*

*Austrian and Serbian Panslavists, the sole object
of which is the weakening of the Triple Alliance
and the destruction of my realm. The efforts of
my Government must in future be directed towards
the isolation and reduction of Serbia. . . . Lasting
peace will, however, be ensured only when Serbia is
eliminated as a factor of political power in the
Balkans. . . . Reconciliation between Serbia and
us is no longer to be thought of, and the continuance
of the peace policy of all European monarchs is
threatened, so long as this hearth fire of criminal
agitation at Belgrade is left unquenched."* Ser-
bophobia—the one and only national hatred to
which the war spirit can appeal in these first days.
This letter brings with it the decision for war, as
hatched out in the past few days by the two Counts
and the Military.

* *

The following noon old Count Szögyény-
Marich, a Hungarian, a good fellow, for many
years Austro-Hungarian Ambassador in Berlin, is
invited to luncheon at Potsdam, there to present
his sovereign's note in person. The Kaiser reads
the long memorandum, then says he must first consult Bethmann, and leads the way in to luncheon.
Here he thaws; the conversation is general; the
Empress is present.

After luncheon the tone changes. Now the Kaiser shows his cards.

"Russia's attitude will, in any case, be hostile. . . . Should war between Austria-Hungary and Russia prove inevitable, Vienna may be sure that Germany, her loyal and tried ally, will stand by the side of the Monarchy. Moreover, Russia just now is in no way prepared for war. . . . I understand perfectly that the Emperor Franz Joseph, in his well-known love of peace, would be reluctant to march into Serbia; but if Vienna has really decided that warlike action against Serbia is necessary, I should regret it if Austria-Hungary neglected the present most favourable opportunity. As to Roumania, I will see to it that King Carol and his advisers observe a correct attitude. . . . I never trusted King Ferdinand an inch, and do not trust him now. . . . Still, I will make no objections whatever to the conclusion of a treaty between the Monarchy and Bulgaria. . . ."

With every sentence the old Hungarian's spirits rise. He hurries home, looks at the cypher manual, and telegraphs the precious words to Vienna.

And yet he has seen only one corner of Wilhelm's soul; the artfully modulated bearing, first stiff, then impulsive. For even before he had any idea of this memorandum, Wilhelm had read in his Ambassador's report from Vienna that the latter had expressly and gravely warned the warlike Counts against overhaste. Then the Kaiser had seized his long pencil with the Imperial crown and written in the margin opposite those sensible words:

"Who authorised him to act in that way? It is very stupid! None of his business. . . . Later, if plans go wrong it will be said that Germany refused! Tschirschky will be good enough to drop this nonsense! The Serbs must be disposed of, and that right soon! Now or never!"

What had excited the Kaiser-Peacemaker so dreadfully? Not two years ago the Serbs were advancing in Albania, with the sea as their ultimate goal. Vienna wanted war; but the Kaiser opposed it. He summarised his ideas in the following memorable passage:

"Austria has incautiously adopted a sharp, dictatorial tone towards Serbia's claims. This may have a provocative effect and lead to complications. Serbia demands access to the Adriatic, with ports; Austria refuses this wish à limine. *Russia seems desirous of supporting the Serb aspirations, and might come into conflict with Austria over this point. . . . Then the* casus fœderis *arises for Germany, Vienna having been attacked by Petersburg —see the treaty. This involves mobilisation, and*

war on two fronts for Germany. . . . Paris will undoubtedly be supported by London. Thus Germany would have to embark on a life-and-death struggle with three great Powers. We hazard all, and may lose all.

"All this because Austria won't have the Serbs in Albania or Durazzo. Obviously that cannot be offered to Germany as a reason for launching her into a death-struggle. There is no conceivable way of getting the German nation to feel enthusiastic over a war waged for such a reason: and no one could reconcile it with his conscience and his responsibility before God and his people if he hazarded Germany's existence for such a cause.

"It would be going far beyond the terms of any treaty to make the German Army and people directly subservient to the foreign policy of another State. This would be tantamount to holding them at its disposition! The Triple Alliance gives the three Signatory States a simply mutual guarantee of their existing territorial integrity; it does not pledge them to unquestioning support in a case of friction over someone else's territory! The casus fœderis does, indeed, arise if Austria is attacked by Russia; but only on condition that Austria has not provoked Russia to attack her. But in this case such a situation might well arise over Serbia,

*and Vienna must avoid that in all circumstances.
Austria must listen to proposals for mediation, or
make them.*

*"Should Russia reject Austrian proposals for
mediation, if acceptable and approved by the other
Powers, she would put herself in the wrong as
against Vienna. She will draw the displeasure of
the Powers on herself and incur the suspicion that
she is trying to provoke war with Austria at any
cost, Albania being only a transparent pretext.
She will be looked on as the peace-breaker, and will
evoke the anger of every sensible man."*

In this document Wilhelm II solved with statesmanlike insight a political conflict analogous in
almost every respect with that of July 1914. The
anticipation that England would come in, the
Bismarckian theory that "the Alliance is not a
mutual benefit society," the all-important point
that Europe would condemn that party which provoked the conflict, the recognition of Serbia's need
of a port—all these points are most justly per-
ceived. He needed only to repeat these words on
July 6, 1914, exactly as he had written them in
this document of November 11, 1912. The sole
decision over peace or war lay, under the Constitution, with the German Kaiser. Had he repeated
his own thoughts on that day, he would have made

WILLIAM II

Emperor of Germany, 1888–1918

it impossible for the Viennese Cabinet to take any action, and would thus have prevented any possibility of the World War breaking out when it did.

His change of front is primarily to be explained —setting aside his psycho-pathological nature— by the thought of the assassination of Royalty. This, too, explains the mood of the War Counts in Vienna. It had been impossible to make war in 1912, in face of the Kaiser's veto; but after the murder they felt that at last the moment had come to enlist him for their plans.

In those twenty intervening months the quarrel had not grown more acute, nor had the alliance become more intimate. If the opposing group had drawn closer together, then there was all the greater need for cautious consideration of any conflict in all its aspects before making Destiny responsible. And yet to-day the Kaiser blackguarded his Ambassador, who had taken exactly his own previous standpoint, as if he were a cabdriver who had taken the wrong road.

Why must Austria and Germany "*dispose of the Serbs, and that right soon*"?

This time a second motive—vanity—is at work in his heart. "*This time they shall see that he does not flinch.*"

Behind this sentence one detects the voices of the Generals, the embarrassed silence of the servile Courtiers, the resigned smile of the Crown Prince, the silent looks of the Admirals, the scornful comments of the Pan-German Press. At each hope for war, followed by each fresh decision of the Kaiser in favour of peace, they one and all give him gently to understand that the glorious army, the strongest force in the world, is standing round him, ready to the last gaiter-button, and yet he dares not.

His vanity was irritated, moreover, in still more intimate fashion. If Bismarck's loyalty to his king was rooted in his faith, as he sometimes used to say, Wilhelm's faith was a product of his sense of kingship. This "by the grace of God!" is certainly the most genuine note in the Kaiser's soul; at the same time, it relieves his mediæval mentality of the necessity of thinking himself one with the people; he stands alone. But, true to his rank, he extends this theory, which originates in his sentiments towards himself, to cover all his crowned kinsmen. And of all the Princes, none was more his friend than Franz Ferdinand, or so at least he thought. And had they dared to shoot this Archduke of the most ancient lineage of Europe: to murder the German Kaiser's friend? By the grace of God and the favour of Wilhelm—and yet slaughtered? He felt it as a personal attack on himself; felt that his honour bound him to avenge the wrong. The War Counts, who could not stir without Wilhelm's sword, had calculated justly.

In the afternoon the Chancellor and Zimmermann, the Under-Secretary of State, are summoned to the Schlosspark at Potsdam. Both agree dutifully with the Kaiser, the more so as the latter, *"without waiting to hear what the Chancellor advised,"* immediately gave his instructions regarding the answer for Vienna; the situation grave, the decision to be left to Austria herself, Roumania not to be offended, Bulgaria's support to be secured, the conflict localised, in the last resort the obligations of alliance. In the evening Bethmann passes on the Kaiser's instructions to the Austrian Ambassador, and adds, on his own account, *"immediate intervention against Serbia is the best solution."* Count Hoyos, sitting by his side, nods eagerly. He is younger and bolder than the old Ambassador, and he has been saying to everyone in the office to-day: *"We shall wipe Serbia out."*

The very next morning heads are cooler. Zimmermann writes a private letter to the German Ambassador in Vienna pointing out the urgent

necessity of warning Austria not to make her
demands too sharp; but this sensible thought remained for ever enshrined in its letter paper, the
paper in the envelope, the envelope in a drawer,
where the writer found it, to his dismay, three
years later, when clearing out his desk before
leaving office. Even Bethmann flinched a little,
for when Zimmermann drew up a report of yesterday's conversations for the Ambassador in Vienna,
and made the Kaiser "stand loyally by Austria's
side under all circumstances," Bethmann ran his
pen through the last three words, and left his
sovereign with "loyalty," simple and unadorned.

The spectacle of Bethmann's advances and re-
treats, his eternal vacillations, will occupy us for
four whole weeks, and three years after that. As
a boy, Bethmann had been at the head of his
school, and even now he reads the Greek classics
in the original for recreation; as a young man he
passed his law examinations brilliantly, achieved a
great social reputation in country-houses and shoot-
ing-parties, and, take him for all in all, exemplified
most admirably Bismarck's epigram that Prussia
produces excellent Privy Councillors and routine
ministers, but no statesmen.

*   *

The next morning—the morning of July 6th—

the Kaiser departs. So we have the Father of the
People churning the Baltic waves, the Secretary of
State honeymooning in Lucerne, Herr von Stumm
sun-bathing at the seaside, the commanders of the
Army and the Fleet enjoying themselves in Carls-
bad and Tarasp, the Quarter-Master-General,
burying an aunt at Hanover, and (a few days
later) the Chancellor retiring to his country-estate,
whence he governs by telephone. Is this the picture
of a Government that is thirsting for war? No one
had gone on leave in Vienna or Petersburg!

The Kaiser saw what might be coming, although
it was none of his wish. But the Chancellor, incited by the Generals, who needed a free hand for
only a few weeks to come to blows, got the Kaiser,
whose true instinct warned him to stay, out of the
way, on the pretext that abandonment of the journey would cause panic abroad. As the danger-
clouds thicken, the Kaiser wishes to make sure that
all preparations are complete. On the same gar-
den-seat, the same afternoon, he receives the Minister of War; early next morning, a representative
of the Chief of the Naval Staff (who is himself absent), a representative of the Chief of the General
Staff, and one of the Secretaries of State for Naval
Affairs. No *"Crown Council"* was ever held—unfortunately; had there been one, the Departmental

Chiefs could have expressed their objections to the Imperial wishes. Falkenhayn's audience is brief. The Kaiser reads him the letter and memorandum from Vienna—presumably only in excerpts, since it occupies twelve pages of typescript. The Minister of War records his impression, *"so far as was possible considering the haste,"* that Vienna is not determined on war; and adds to Moltke: *"So your Excellency need not, presumably, cut your cure short."*

Next morning the Kaiser, all ready for his journey, receives the other three gentlemen in the Palace Park with equal expedition. He tells Capelle, representing the Admiral of the Fleet (on leave): *"I do not believe in any serious warlike developments. The Tsar will not place himself on the side of regicides. Besides, neither Russia nor France is prepared for war. Being anxious not to create any uneasiness, I shall, on the Chancellor's advice, start on my trip north. I wanted merely to inform you of the strained situation, in order that you may consider what is to follow."*

Not one of the four responsible representatives of the German military and naval commands was asked his opinion. These high officers are there only to receive and reproduce the commands of the Supreme War Lord; there is no consultation between them. The Minister of War has to make a hurried guess at Austria's intentions; and he guesses wrong, because the fundamental document on which the whole threat of war depends is not even shown him. At the same time, the Kaiser is wrong about the enemy; no wonder, since everything is still in embryo. Only one trifle is already certain: the German Army and Fleet—in other words, the lives of ten million men—are pledged by the word of one Emperor to another, and two Counts in Vienna have from to-day on *"a free hand"* to hazard them wherever their frivolity and folly deem fit.

Then the *Hohenzollern* puts to sea, the Kaiser—out of reach except through wireless—sees only water, air, and the faces of his parasites: and so for three long weeks, during which, on dry land, countless personal conversations between statesmen are shaping the destiny of Europe.

CHAPTER III

THE ULTIMATUM

NEXT morning the ministers of the Monarchy are sitting round the Council table at the Ballplatz. Count Berchtold has received the gentlemen, allotting the places with careful ceremony, as at a great dinner-party. He himself makes the most elegant of presidents—it is his great moment. On his right hand sits the fine figure of Count Tisza, with his inscrutable expression; on his left a tall man with a grey pointed beard, rather like Bethmann, but healthier looking, Count Stürgkh, a nobleman from Styria and Minister-President of Austria-Hungary—but how he came to occupy that position, neither he nor history knows. His weather-beaten features are flanked by the pale, foxy face of the Pole, Ritter von Bilinski, who knows everything that is going on in the Monarchy, and rather too much of what is going on among its enemies; perhaps the most

dangerous man at this table, where four nationalities and five ministries are sitting in mutual dis-
trust.

These four diplomats, these four grizzled civilians, are about to throw themselves into the arms of
the three splendid gentlemen in green, white, and
gold, who are seated with them at the table. These
are the Imperial and Royal Minister of War, Von
Krobatin—a sergeant-major's head with a Balkan
moustache; an Admiral representing the naval command; and Freiherr Conrad von Hötzendorf, the
principal figure—the man who reformed the Austrian Army and planned a campaign against Italy,
undoubtedly the chief embodiment of the pride and
warlike spirit of the Monarchy. His features indi-
cate decision and energy, but too much self-renunci-
ation. It is the head of a thinker, rather than a
soldier; and the head of a man whose effect on
women is stronger than on men.

Count Berchtold, having made all the preparations required by ceremony, opens this Council of
War by remarking that its object is to advise on
the measures *"to be taken to meet the dangerous
internal political situation which the catastrophe of
Sarajevo has revealed as existing in Bosnia and
Herzegovina."* Then he announces his intention
"of putting an end to Serbian intrigues once and

for all by an enunciation of power." Germany's
collaboration is *"solemnly and most emphatically
promised."* A decisive stroke, a settlement of accounts, and then the open confession: *"I realize
that war with Russia is a very probable consequence
of the Serbian war."* (Later on the Count alters
this all-important sentence in the Protocol with his
own hand to the less uncompromising wording *"that
a campaign against Serbia might have war with
Russia as its consequence."*)

Count Tisza opposes: *"I shall never consent to
anything like a surprise-attack upon Serbia without previous diplomatic action, such as seems to be
intended. It is absolutely necessary that we should
formulate demands which may be hard, but must
not be impossible to fulfil. If Serbia accepts them,
we shall be able to point to a brilliant diplomatic
success, and our prestige in the Balkans will rise.
If Serbia refuses, I agree that we should take military measures, but I must point out at once that we
must not aim at the absolute annihilation of Serbia.
Russia would fight to the death before allowing this,
and I, as Hungarian Minister-President, should
never consent to the Monarchy's annexing part of
Serbia."* Furthermore, war was at this moment
both unnecessary and dangerous.

Thereupon both Stürgkh and Bilinski speak in

favour of war, both basing their opinions on Potiorek's ingenious memorandum (he hopes to cut the
knot of the internal difficulties in Bosnia with the
sword). The Minister of War agrees with the
majority, with the phrase—as stupid as it is typical
—"*A diplomatic success is valueless.*" He expressly
recommends a preventive war, but is in favour of
striking at once; and adds ingeniously: "*From a
military point of view I must point out that it
would be better to go to war now than later. . . . We
have already lost two opportunities. If we do not
strike now, this will be taken in the Southern Slav
provinces as a sign of weakness.*" Count Stürgkh
goes a step farther still, to cover all events, and
suggests: "*It would probably be well to remove
the reigning family in Belgrade and give the crown
to an European prince.*"

Count Tisza's fighting-spirit grows with opposition. When the War Counts and Knights insist
unanimously on unacceptable demands to Serbia,
Hungary grows threatening: "*I have met you,
gentlemen, so far as to concede that the demands
should be very hard. If, however, our intention of
proposing unacceptable terms is undisguised, we
shall be in an impossible situation legally for declaring war. If my point of view is disregarded in the
note, I shall draw the consequences.*" Then he turns

on Bilinski, and declares that he is partly responsible for the Sarajevo murder.

Now it is the turn of the military. The Minister of War states that a war on three fronts is possible. The balance of forces and the *"probable course of a European war"* are considered. They part, still undecided.

Will Count Tisza's firm attitude avert the catastrophe?

*　　*

Von Tschirschky-Bögendorff, the German Ambassador in Vienna, was shrewd, unobtrusive, cautious, a man of some education, good-natured, and not wholly old-fashioned. He looked the part, too, with his clerkly face, in which everything was very refined—hair, glance, and even voice. He had once been Secretary of State, but had afterwards moved down again. He was even more anxious to preserve respect for his position than for his person; was not vain, and improved on acquaintance.

His only grudge was against the Court of Petersburg: he had been insulted there. As a matter of fact, he was too stiff for harum-scarum Russian Society, and once at a Court ball a Grand Duke had been so careless as to annex his supper-partner.

There followed complaints, apologies, and his transfer. He will never forget that moment; his mistrustful nature sees in it a plot, anti-German feeling—of which, indeed, there were plenty of other and more important manifestations.

For all that, his first step in this crisis was to warn against over-hasty decisions. *"It should be kept in mind that Austria-Hungary does not stand alone in the world, that it is her duty to take into consideration the entire European situation."* This wise sentence earned him a snub from the Kaiser in the shape of a marginal note, which was passed on to him from Berlin translated into a reproof for "slackness." This came on top of the old grudge against Petersburg and a complete indifference to politics in his Embassy, which employed two princes more interested in music than in politics. The Ambassador would have done better to resign, instead of playing the strong man in obedience to Berlin. He remained at his post, and fell into line.

Towards Berchtold he entertained, not only the mistrust usual among allies, but that natural to his character; nevertheless, he called on the Minister and declared: *"In the name of my Imperial Master I inform you emphatically that Berlin expects the Monarchy to take action against Serbia and Ger-*

many would not understand it" if Vienna failed to
act. His Saxon tongue had suddenly become
Prussian.

Immediately Berchtold writes out these precious words for his enemy Tisza, the conventional
"du" lending them extra spice. Tisza, however,
remains unmoved. Or rather, he writes urgently
to the Emperor explaining his point of view.

The Emperor, however, was 84 years old; and
Berchtold's elegant, forensic fluency was more effective than any letter from the absent Hungarian.
Accordingly, while Tisza was expounding his
peaceful policy in Budapest, amid the unanimous
applause of the Hungarian Ministers, Franz
Joseph approved his Foreign Minister's plan of
war.

When Count Tisza comes to Vienna a week later
he is suddenly another man. What has so transformed him, soul and brain? Perhaps he hopes that
the war will be over in a year and win him the elections, which threaten to grow dangerous to the oli-
garchy of Budapest, despite the millions of crowns
spent on bribery. Perhaps his heart has been
touched by the prayers of his cousins, the feudal
agrarians, who see in the murder of their future
sovereign a glorious opportunity to wage war
against their dangerous rival, the Serbian pig.

Further, there are small personal jealousies which have prevented him from consulting the Opposition, even confidentially, in this extraordinary situation.

One thing is certain, that in the meantime he has read a threatening document—an urgent appeal to the Foreign Minister from the Chief of the General Staff, who abstains, indeed, from interfering in political decisions, *"only I must again point out, as I have already explained by word of mouth, in complete agreement with your Excellency, that in taking diplomatic steps everything must be avoided which might allow delay, or successive repetitions of the diplomatic action, thus giving the enemy time to make his military preparations . . . if, however, the decision to make the* démarche *stands, military interests demand that this should be carried through in a single action with a short time-limit for the Ultimatum."*

The intention is plain, and has its effect. The voice of the General is heard threatening the Diplomat, at the orders of that Diplomat himself, who hopes by this ruse to overcome the Hungarian's hesitation. This letter refers clearly to confidential conversations; indeed, it was written so hurriedly that even the date was omitted and only added conjecturally in after-years. For a whole fortnight Tisza has to listen daily to the same phrases: "prestige, enunciation of power, signs of weakness, making a clean sweep, action"; on top of this, reiterated fanfares from Berlin and the prizes which Berchtold was never weary of dangling before him: the strongest army in Europe on one's side, a completely "free hand" in Berlin. Finally, unveiled threats from the supreme military authorities; "you will be responsible to us for the consequences of delay!" The most convinced pacifist would have found that hard to resist; how much more an officer, a man living at that day and in that circle of feudal aristocrats.

Thus the last internal enemy of the War Counts was worn down by suggestion. Tisza visits the German Ambassador and declares himself converted to the Ultimatum. The next day he makes a statement in the Budapest Parliament which is so equivocal that even the Paris *Temps* praises his moderation.

In Vienna, where there is no Parliament to disturb the circles of war-mongers, public opinion is being manipulated all the more vigorously. A large portion of the Press is fulminating against Serbia, against that *"gang of robbers and murderers,"* the *"sheep-stealers,"* the *"nation of lice."* By the middle of the month the violence is far greater than at the beginning; and since the Bel-

© Scherls Bilderienst

COUNT STEPHAN TISZA, OF HUNGARY
Member of the Cabinet of the Austrian Emperor

grade papers answer in just the same way, the question arises, who began it. Let it not be answered here, or ever; it is the Delphic riddle of the war, for which any solution suits and none suffices.

The Counts, indeed, go about their work in profound secrecy, like Freemasons, so that even the Serbian Minister in Vienna can do no more than report, as he does continually, that something is in the air; but he cannot say what. Hötzendorf, in his letter, has recommended *"avoiding everything that might prematurely alarm our antagonists; on the contrary, every show should be made of absolutely peaceful intentions."* To postpone the performance suddenly till to-morrow and then give it to-day after all—that is their idea of cleverness.

"Have you heard anything?" the foreign diplomats ask one another when they meet at Sacher's (for the usual weekly reception at Berchtold's has stopped). And although they hear nothing, they discover all sorts of things; they guess, put two and two together, criticise.

"I assure you, Your Excellency, there is only one person who knows anything at all; that is Tschirschky, and he will not say."

"They say Stürgkh is looking worried."

"I saw Brudermann driving past; he was beaming."

"Shebeko said openly that he would back Serbia up if anything happened."

"Is not Shebeko going on leave to-morrow? If so, he cannot be expecting anything very bad."

"Dumaine merely smiles."

"Dumaine always smiles."

Yes, Tschirschky holds his tongue because he does not know much; for the secret is being kept even from Berlin itself. What a mercy that the Germans answered a courteous, general question as to what they thought about the Ultimatum with a sweeping gesture: "That was Austria's affair!" How can they be expected to have time and attention for such things to-day, when quite another problem is occupying the Foreign Office in Berlin; namely, ought one to telegraph to the King of Serbia for his birthday to-morrow or not? The Ultimatum? Purely Austria's concern! In the very ante-chamber of the World War the courtly diplomats of the Imperial capitals step back politely at the door and say, in chorus, "After you, Your Excellency!"

For all that, it is reported to Berlin that the demands will probably include the issue of a manifesto by King Peter denouncing the Greater Serbia movement; a general inquiry into the responsibility, Austria participating; and the dismissal of all persons in Belgrade proved to be compromised. The substance but not the text of these three demands is known to Bethmann in Hohenfinow, to Jagow in Berlin, to Tirpitz in Tarasp, and to the Kaiser at sea, in anything from eleven to five days before the Ultimatum; but no one grows mistrustful, no one asks for explanations or for the exact wording.

On the contrary, the Austrian Ambassador reports from Berlin to Vienna: "*His Majesty and all others in authority are encouraging us most emphatically to act against Serbia with all energy, and to clear out that nest of revolutionary conspirators once for all. They leave the choice of means entirely to the judgment of the Monarchy. It is hardly too much to say that they are putting pressure on us to act.*" Berchtold assures him that "*There can be no question of hesitation or indecision here.*" The final draft will, in any case, be sent to the German Government before it is acted upon.

But shadows soon fall on the war fervour in Vienna. "Supposing these Serbian bandits are so disobliging as to accept everything?" "*Then it would have to be made clear,*" the Bavarian Minister writes to his Court, "*whether the intention of destroying Serbia is unalterable. They do not, however, propose to let this second decision arise at all. They will make the contents of the note quite impossible of acceptance. . . . It is thought that if Russia refuses to allow the struggle to be local- ised, the present moment is more favourable for set- tling accounts than any later one."*

Suicide from fear or death, as Bismarck said.

* * *

These and similar reports awaken uneasiness in the Berlin Cabinet. A sensible man is at his post again. As he is by no means a romantic—not even after his honeymoon—he seems bent on becoming a cynic. Herr von Jagow has risen to be Secretary of State: a smallish man with the hard, colourless features of the specialist—a face behind which the formation of the skull seems to show through; a man without illusions, but also without many pre- judices; a realist, cautious, and with a knowledge of human nature.

Jagow at once sees the danger involved in the Kaiser's blank cheque, and says to Krupp von Boh- len: *"I should never have acted like that. But since the Kaiser has determined on his attitude in ad- vance, it is now too late to take any further steps against Vienna."* A classical presentment of the main question: a voice of doubt at last from the

Wilhelmstrasse! But even Jagow does not go to the Kaiser and say: "Sire, I can no longer serve you"; he takes on him the heritage of July 5th, the day on which the Kaiser had prescribed his policy to the Chancellor.

But Jagow has ideas. In this crisis he begs Berlin to send a warning to Haldane, to reinforce any resistance there may be in the Cabinet, especially from Grey, to a possible naval agreement with Russia. On the main point he speaks like the rest. This is the feeling of the Office immediately before the Note, as described by the Bavarian Minister:

"A powerful and successful move against Serbia would make it possible for the Austrians and Hungarians to feel themselves once more a national power . . . For this reason it was here unhesitatingly declared that we would agree to any method of procedure which might be determined on there, even at the risk of a war with Russia. . . . In Vienna they do not seem to have expected such unconditional support of the Danube Monarchy by Germany, and one has the impression that it is almost embarrassing to the always timid and undecided authorities at Vienna not to be admonished by Germany to caution and self-restraint. . . . In the interests of the localisation of the war, the Imperial

*German Government will initiate diplomatic action
at the Courts of all the Great Powers immediately
upon the presentation of the Austrian Note in Belgrade. It will claim that the Austrian action has
been just as much of a surprise to it as to the other
Powers, pointing out the fact that the Kaiser is
away travelling in the north, and that the Prussian
Minister of War, as well as the Chief of the Grand
General Staff, is on leave of absence. . . .*

*"German troops are not to be mobilised, and our
military authorities are also to use their influence to
prevent Austria from mobilising her entire forces,
particularly not those troops stationed in Galicia, in
order to avoid bringing about automatically a
counter-mobilisation on the part of Russia, which
would force, first ourselves, and then France, to
take similar measures, and thereby conjure up a
European war. . . . If, however, it comes to war
after all, opinion here is that we should find our
English cousins on the side of our enemies. . . ."*

And after assigning its precise rôle to every
State in Europe, this devastating diplomatic document closes with a Parisian jest.

The ship of state glides down the stream, a slender pleasure-boat, between whirlpools and preci-
pices. No one really cares to take the oars, only

from time to time a hand reaches to the rudder to prevent the craft from running ashore. None of the German diplomats wants a European war: in his heart each one of them hopes that the whole business will be quietly settled, for, as the report says, *"thanks to her indecision and desultoriness, Austria-Hungary has now become the real 'sick man' of Europe. It is therefore doubtful whether Vienna will really decide on action."* Thus one Empire doubts the other's resolution, while the other in its turn takes fright when it finds its plans encouraged by the first. Each wishes the other to put obstacles in its way, making action impossible, but throwing the consequences of inaction on the other. As neither is quite confident in its own decisions, it trusts to the other, and hopes that the enemy's unwillingness may help them both out of their difficulty.

From time to time Jagow sits up in the boat as it is carried down the stream—the boat which he ought to be steering—and ventures a question. He asks Vienna, timidly, *"What are the ideas of Austria-Hungary's statesmen concerning the future status of Serbia? . . . It would be useful to us to be informed to a certain extent as to where the road is likely to lead us."*

But the wily Viennese have no intention of put-

ting the infamy they are planning in black
and white, and showing it to their friends before
it is irrevocable. They put off the German Ambassador, always promising to tell him to-morrow. The
Baron whom the Foreign Ministry keeps to draw
up its ultimatums and similar manifestoes has to
rewrite the note four times before the Ministerial
Council approves it. Here there comes another
conflict with Tisza, who seeks to safeguard his
Hungary from Austria at the very beginning by
a formal renunciation of any territorial aggrandisement; just as a Crown Prince on the point of a
misalliance has to renounce his children's rights before begetting them. When Berchtold announces
his intention of partitioning the greater part of
Serbia among her neighbours, Tisza canvasses the
whole plan energetically. Count Stürgkh reverts
to his favourite idea of deposing the Serbian dynasty. The Count has some objection to this family. Finally they agree on retaining, at most, only
certain strategical points.

And is it thus, Count Berchtold, that your
dearest enemy would filch, before the first shot is
fired, the choicest morsels of that great booty for
the sake of which you are destroying the peace of
Europe? But the Minister smiles a Metternich-
like smile. A Minister proposes to conquer an

enemy country. His colleague has reason to fear
that such an enlargement of the common Fatherland would strengthen the other's half; therefore
Tisza insures himself against the imminent danger
of a victory, and bathes himself and his reluctant
confrères in rays of peace and morality. He is for
chastening the criminals only, not for despoiling
them.

* *

At last the note is ready. It is very long, and
begins by demanding from the Serbian King a declaration in set terms denouncing all Greater Serbia
agitations, to be published without delay in the
official organ, like the verdict in the Press at the
close of a libel action. Then follow ten demands,
five of them directed against the agitation: sup-
pression of all propaganda in the Press and
associations; dissolution of the Narodna Obrana;
supervision of instruction in schools; dismissal of
all officers and officials compromised—their names
to be communicated from Vienna; and the participation of the Imperial and Royal Governments in
the investigation. Apparently general proscrip-
tion is still possible, as enacted by Austria and
Prussia in concert a hundred years ago in the
Karlsbad Decrees, to prevent any union of Ger-

man races and German states. Then come the
points relating to the murder, and the inquiry, Austrian officials participating.

These are the principal points of the Ultimatum.
Before it was despatched, Count Forgátch hurriedly took a pencil and made it a little more veno-
mous still. State institutions, opinions, sentiments,
are summoned in peremptory fashion to appear before a Court which is judge in its own cause, forty-
eight hours being allowed for unconditional acceptance. The note is to be delivered at Belgrade at
such a moment that when its contents are telegraphed to Petersburg, the French President, who
is just finishing his visit there, will no longer be
present to hear them. The time-table is worked
out. At the last moment Jagow learns that Poincaré is not leaving Petersburg in the afternoon,
but only in the evening. Berchtold accordingly puts
off the delivery of the note by one hour. So the
two work, one slender shoulder against the other;
and the German occupies himself with the hour of
presentation of a note, the contents of which he
does not know, but for which he has promised his
nation's support. The two are united by the truly
statesmanlike thought that the French and Russians must not be allowed to discuss it together;
the Frenchman must be on the high seas when he

gets the message. Count Berchtold's concoction is
to be acid, with an additional relish of unexpected-
ness: a *note à la surprise.* He knows that this ome-
lette, his masterpiece, means an ultimatum to Europe. His old Emperor, too, sees clearly. After
reading the ultimatum, he says to Bilinski: *"Russia
cannot accept this. . . . It is no use shutting one's
eyes; this means a big war!"*

The Serbs are to read it on Thursday evening,
after nearly a month's whispering has made both
countries nervous and their Presses hysterical. Two
days earlier, the German Ambassador in Vienna
has the document in his hands at last. Is he not
shocked? Does he not hurry to the telephone, report
fully to his chiefs in Berlin, and ask authority to
prevent its being despatched in this form?

He does not even telegraph it, it is really too
long to encode. In any case, the Austrians will
pass it on to-morrow, and one might "compro-
mise one's cypher" by sending in it a document
that the whole world is going to read so soon.

So the decisive twenty-four hours are wasted.

It is only on the following afternoon that the
old Hungarian Count in Berlin, having obviously
been recommended by his chief in Vienna to delay
till the last moment, brings the paper to the German Secretary of State. Now Jagow, who knew

only that the blank cheque was being filled in, but
not for how much, sees the total that the Kaiser
had guaranteed in the dark, a fortnight previously,
without asking advice. He says anxiously: *"That's
pretty sharp!"* Thereupon the old Count answers
with these classic words: *"Well, there's nothing
more to be done about it. To-morrow morning it
will be handed in at Belgrade in that form!"*

"Well, there's nothing more to be done," thinks
Jagow. "Nothing more," thinks Bethmann, whose
tongue not even the Viennese pepper can loosen.
Do they not realise that the old Hungarian is
lying to them, even on the point of the hour of
presentation? And even if this is merely his mistake, why do they not intervene this same evening? The Kaiser on his ship could not, indeed, be
reached so quickly; but in half an hour they could
be talking to Vienna, and Vienna could be talking
to its Minister in Belgrade within two hours. Bethmann, Jagow, Zimmermann, agree in describing
the note as *"In every respect too sharp"*; but none
of them thinks of altering the circular note telegraphed yesterday and to-day to the German Ambassadors in Petersburg, Paris, and London, to
guide the decisive negotiations in the Cabinets of
those capitals the day after to-morrow. This communication states that Germany considers her ally's

note (which they had not yet seen) to be *"moderate and proper."* Now the gentlemen leave this unconditional approval of the Ultimatum officially standing before Europe; although condemning the note, they step in protectingly between Austria and Europe.

But when, a few days later, someone spoke to Count Berchtold of the danger of his Ultimatum, he wagged his manicured finger in the air with a gently admonitory gesture, slightly shook his wearied head, and courteously corrected: *"Pardon, Your Excellency, this is not an ultimatum; it is a dé-*marche *with a time-limit."*

CHAPTER IV

DISMAY

ON a hard inn bed in a Serbian hamlet lies a grizzled man with a reckless face; dark, furrowed, scarred by life, but indomitable. He has just made perhaps his thousandth electoral speech, accompanied by the cheers of his Party friends, and has come back to rest. To-morrow morning he must travel on. He is weary to death of dust and heat, of phrase-making and heckling, and yet he cannot relax. The man is Pashitch, Minister-President of Serbia.

"It must come soon now," he thinks, staring at the wall. "It cannot be more than a few days longer. And this damned electoral campaign coming at this moment! In Vienna they can take things easier. His Majesty says the word, the Court stands at attention, summer-quarters whenever possible, and so long as the august forehead is not clouded, the Minister suns himself in favour. We poor chaps are run off our legs, touting for the

so-called popular favour. Like those Romans
whom I saw once in that play of Shakespeare's—
what was its name?—when I was studying engi-
neering at Zürich.

"Thirty years Radical leader, and still touring
the country at elections! I believe I was really
freer as a young refugee in Bulgaria and Switzer-
land. There was a price on my head, of course,
but no one bothered me. Will Russia keep her
word this time? The Tsar promised me faithfully
last year: *'Tell your King that we will do everything for Serbia!'* But what does the poor chap
know about politics? Isvolski is gone, Hartwig's
dead, Sazonov isn't safe."

And between sleeping and waking his mind reviews for the hundredth time the coils of the last
few days, out of which his plans are taking form.
Possibly he thinks of Bismarck; he, too, needed
three wars to unite all the branches of his nation.
He, Pashitch, had just come through two; his country had been almost doubled; its old enemies, Bulgaria and Turkey, were beaten. If now, with
Russia's help, he could bring down the ramshackle
Monarchy, the last Southern Slavs would unite
with Serbia and the ambition of 15,000,000 men,
the dream of five centuries, would be fulfilled!
Bismarck, the great enemy of his nation, who had

taken Bosnia away from Turkey at his Congress
in Berlin and yet had not restored it to the Serbs—
this very Bismarck had always been his model!
Bismarck conquered two provinces—which were
only half German at that—from the French. Why
should not we do the same by Austria with two
others which are entirely ours by race and not even
legally Austria's?

"That haughty Count from Vienna never winks
an eyelid and calmly pockets two provinces which
he was supposed to be administering under European supervision. How did the Turkish Revolution give him more of a right than us? You forced
us to beg your pardon because you had stolen a
piece of land from the Turks, but our thoughts are
free! There are enough nations in Europe who
have won their liberty by fighting Austria!"

A knock on the door rouses him from these
thoughts. A telegram from Belgrade. Austria's
Ultimatum. Back home at once!

*   *

Three weeks earlier, and three hours after the
murder, when the news exploded in Belgrade like
a bomb, the cleverest man in the city had said:
"God grant it wasn't a Serb!" The speaker was
himself no Serb, and his pious invocation was a

sham, for he had been longing for this war for years and trying to provoke a conflict; he hoped to lead Russia victorious into Vienna from Belgrade. This was Von Hartwig, the Russian Minister, a conspicuous figure, seeing that his master, the Tsar, was the lodestar of all Serbian hopes. On the evening of the murder he entertained guests; on that evening the Russian Legation was lit up in festal fashion.

The next day Hartwig goes across to his Austrian colleague. Excellency presses Excellency's sympathetic hand in silent hostility.

"Soon we shall be squaring accounts," thinks the Austrophobe.

"Scoundrels," thinks the Russophobe.

The next moment Hartwig falls from his chair, and in two minutes he is dead.

"Extremely awkward, this happening here!" thinks the young Baron, blind to the symbolic character of the scene. Will the nations understand it?

The first days after the murder all circles in Belgrade were very much depressed. Only a few weeks ago the murderers had been here; it was here that Serbian officers and officials had helped to supply them with weapons. Vague rumours of an impending assassination had reached the Govern-

ment. It was felt that the world, and above all
the enemy, would hold Serbia morally responsible.
Moreover, economic negotiations with the Monarchy were just on the point of conclusion. The
whole of the Balkans groaned as in a nightmare
throughout July. Again the feeling awoke of two
races and two cultures in collision, while two military Powers stood behind them. The ancient rivalry between Austria and Russia kept the fires
smouldering in this corner of Europe. At first the
newspapers condemned the murder; but on the
very next day the Serbian Minister in Petersburg
tactlessly and foolishly announced in the Press that
the crime was due to the discontent in Bosnia.
Then the fireworks began simultaneously in Vienna
and Belgrade. There was no retreat now, and a
torrent of abuse spurted from the Press, unchecked
by either Government, since each enjoyed seeing
itself lit up by the Bengal fire.

On the fatal day all was ready in the Austrian
Legation. Giesl, the Minister, had been rehears-
ing his attitude for the historical moment since
the early morning. His master's orders ran, "between 4 and 5 o'clock." Suddenly comes a telegram from Vienna; as Poincaré will not be leaving
Petersburg until 11 o'clock, Giesl is to present the
note *"a few minutes before 5, at the earliest,"* and

to telegraph at once whether he will act at 5, or wait till 6. Giesl's excitement rises. Sometimes a people's destiny hangs on an hour; and although all he has to do is to telephone that he is going at 6, he does not abandon his tragedian's rôle, and wires that he will make every effort not to carry the *démarche* through until 6 o'clock. The heritage of Metternich!

At 6 o'clock the Ultimatum is presented. The Minister of Finance represents Pashitch: *"It will hardly be possible to convoke the full Ministerial Council so soon; some of the Ministers are away."*

Giesl smiles: *"In the era of railways, telegraphs, and telephones, it should be managed without difficulty in a Kingdom of this size."* Historical words.

*   *

The effect is fearful. In two hours the whole town knows it: "Austria means to destroy us." Crowds throng the streets. Every rumour has a hearing, every leader in turn is reported dead, dismissed, banished. All wish to reject the Ultimatum; but their spirit sinks, for they feel themselves helpless.

The next morning Pashitch arrives, and holds consultations till the evening without reaching a decision. He does, however, show presence of mind. He makes the Crown Prince telegraph to Rome, and most urgently to Petersburg, where the contents of the note have been known since that morning, that he is defenceless, and appeals to the Tsar's Slavonic sympathies.

In the evening the voices of two great Powers are suddenly raised at the Council table; they are heard by the terrified Serbs as those of gods. London advises acceptance of the terms so far as is at all possible; the advice of Paris—although this is only the personal opinion of the acting chargé d'affaires at the Quai d'Orsay—is to try to gain time and appeal to the arbitration of Europe. But the Russian Colossus is silent.

Next day, when the answer can be delayed no longer, there is still no word from Russia, and spirits are low indeed. Pashitch himself advises peace. The people is exhausted after two wars, the dynasty and the Radical Party alike are in a precarious position; the peasants and the officers, heroes of the last victories, are hostile to the Radicals. Timid or cautious, King Peter had for that reason relinquished the conduct of affairs in May, and the Crown Prince was now Regent.

Pashitch advises acceptance to the extreme limit of what is possible, i. e. almost unconditionally.

Eight points are accepted, although in some cases with considerable reservation; even the humiliating clause regarding the Serbian Army is agreed to. All that is asked for is proof of guilt before prosecutions are undertaken, but the participation of Austrian officials in the inquiry is rejected as contrary to the Constitution and the criminal code. In points of detail a false simplicity is affected: how is this to be done, or what does that mean?

While the answer is being submitted to a final revision, a false rumour of an encouraging telegram from the Tsar runs through the town. Feeling changes suddenly, the Army demands war, there is hubbub in the streets. The Crown Prince, walking on foot with his officers, is cheered, but turns into the Palace. Disappointment. Messengers hurry from one Legation to another. *Evvivas* for Italy. Disappointment. Procession to the French Legation, where the young Attaché can find nothing to say to the crowd beyond *"sympathie."* Procession to the British Legation, which has nothing to say at all. Telegrams from Russia to every conceivable person in Belgrade are not delivered, but are stuck up open at the Post Office. They are all encouraging. Fresh processions to the Palace: *"Down with Austria! Woe to all cowards!"* The Crown Prince loses control. Only

wise old Pashitch keeps his head, for the Tsar is
silent. He diplomatically leaves both roads open,
and if he shuts one door of the Temple of Janus
by accepting the Ultimatum, he opens the other
at the same time, and orders general mobilisation.

One o'clock. King Peter sits before the fatal
paper, the first to read what is soon to be laid before a dozen Heads of States. His people have
hardly drawn breath, and now he must call it to
arms again.

Murder brought him to the throne eleven years
ago; the Russian Minister looked on at the window while the last Obrenovitch was butchered opposite. At last the duel of the two dynasties was
over, but like Banquo's ghost it reappears to the
old man in his hours of destiny. England has advised moderation. Is this still the same England
which of old recalled its Minister just because King
Peter had foreknowledge of his enemy's murder?
Much was smoothed over afterwards, but the old
man still feels that he is disliked. The Tsar is
great! He refused, indeed, to give his daughter;
but he is mighty, and he hates Austria.

Peter signs the edict of mobilisation. A Court
train is made up, the gold reserve and the archives
are put on it, and at 3 o'clock the Royal Family

and the Government leave the capital, which lies
on the Austrian frontier, for the interior of Serbia.
The fortress, the station, the city are all in movement; the garrison leaves the walls, munitions are
transported, all goes southward towards Nish.

Suddenly there appears a sight which brings the
terrors of war nearer home to every heart than the
false romanticism of the troops with their music
and flags: the first hospital trains, appearing like
confessors before the sin has been committed, in
silent admonition.

Meanwhile, the Austrian has packed up house-
hold and office effects, and is standing ready in his
travelling clothes in sure and certain hope of a rejection, when, shortly before 6 o'clock, Pashitch
comes over on foot to hand in Serbia's answer.

A few days later Kaiser Wilhelm wrote in the
margin of this document from the hated regicides,
"A brilliant achievement for a time-limit of only 48
*hours . . . with this every reason for war drops
away, and Giesl might have remained quietly in
Belgrade. On the strength of this I should never
have ordered mobilisation!"*

So sensible was the reaction of the German
Kaiser. Vienna, however, had given strict orders
to bring back a *casus belli,* dead or alive. Moreover,
Giesl has no time left in which to read the long

document carefully; he skims it through, sees sundry "ifs" and "buts," feels relieved, and sends the answer, which is ready waiting, across to the Ministry so promptly that the messenger arrives on Pashitch's heels. Relations broken off. Reading and reply alone would have taken an hour; but Giesl is a record-breaker—thirty-five minutes after receipt of the Serbian note the express was carrying him and his suite over the great railway bridge to Semlin, in Austrian territory. For an hour he was the most important man in Europe.

In the same hour, at the Johannistor in Jena, the last of the three "peace poplars," planted one hundred years ago at the Congress of Vienna, crashed to the ground.

CHAPTER V

A N open car dashes from the sea through the light summer night towards the city. In wide curves it sweeps round the port and leaves it, making for the capital. In wide curves the thoughts of its distinguished occupant circle round the port and the two ships on which farewells, accompanied by many promises, have just been exchanged. He sees the national ship send a farewell rocket into the air; sees the gleaming foreign cruiser answer, as it steers slowly westward, making for the Finnish gulf.

For now we are before the gates of Petersburg, and this is the Foreign Minister of the Tsar, who, after four days' brilliant feasting and serious discussions, has just bidden farewell to his ally, the President of France. Blurred like the houses on either hand, the pictures of these last days flit by him. He cannot hold them fast, his memory rushes on like the rushing car.

Sazonov thinks:

"Curiously cool, the public was. I wonder whether the Frenchmen realised that the cheering was all ordered beforehand? I wonder whether they noticed that the workmen were singing revolutionary songs and waving red handkerchiefs? I wager their pockets were full of stones. What could one do? Could one treat the Frenchmen to a massacre? His Majesty behaved well; nobody noticed how his guest's pretensions irritated him; the man behaved more like a monarch than an ordinary business-like President. The affair at the reception of the Diplomatic Corps was really too tactless! This good Poincaré ought to have felt that he was a guest here, and not in a position to snub a foreign Ambassador: *Do not forget, Your Excellency, Serbia has friends in the world who will not leave her in the lurch.* All well and good, but that sort of thing isn't said, certainly not to a man like that Hungarian, who looks down his nose and thinks: 'You are just a party-leader, and I have thirty-two ancestors in direct line!'

"The scarlet escort mightily impressed him. Did he feel the irony of it, when he and his Socialist Minister drove into the fortress of Peter and Paul surrounded by our resplendent Cossacks? *The people outside,* says Paléologue, *were asking whether it was not to the State Prison that they*

were conducting these two revolutionaries.' At
moments such as that the paradox of our alliance
really makes one laugh."

Sazonov's car has reached the high road. As he
speeds along he sees the landscape, lit by the full
moon, stand out clear from the heavy mass of the
great city, and for a few seconds he is absorbed by
the beauty of this summer night. But his brain is
working by night as by day, and all his schemes of
recent years awake within him. Once again his
plans are drawing near to culmination, as two years
ago, when they forged the Balkan alliance. Then
the secret treaty which he initiated made the Tsar
arbiter of the Balkans, and the Treaty of Racco-
nigi bloomed and bore fruit.

"Things were on the verge of coming off"—so
his thoughts ran on. "Italy had her Tripoli, and
now it was our turn to rob Turkey's corpse; the
head of the Caliph on a golden charger! The Straits
were within our grasp; the Tsaritsa dreamed of the
glorious moment when the Kyrie Eleison should
ring once again, after so many centuries, in the
dome of Santa Sophia; and the Tsar shut his ears
to Count Fredericks and the other idealists, and
signed the orders for more ships in the Black Sea.
Only that damned Caillaux made the bankers in
Paris restive, and spoilt Isvolski's work.

"Pashitch won't be sleeping now, either. When he was here last he went pretty far: *'Your Majesty's daughter, at the side of the Serbian Crown Prince, would become Tsaritsa of the Southern Slav Empire.'* Balkan blather. Damned peasant that he is, the idea of procuring a daughter of the Tsar of all the Russias tickles him.

"For all that, the Serbian visit did some good," thinks Sazonov. "The memorandum our General Staff then drew up was able to point out the real importance of an attack by Serbia on Austria: *'For Austria would then be forced to detach four or five corps against Serbia. In the heart of every Russian the Straits have so enormous an import that in any change in the present situation we should be forced to intervene. A campaign against Constantinople will, indeed, hardly be possible, except as part of a European war.'* "

Sazonov's car enters the suburbs: he hears gunshots.

"Still firing?" he thinks uncomfortably. "Eighty-three thousand strikers. In the Viborg quarter they have even gone to the length of putting up barricades. And at the same time our Imperial Guard was playing the Frenchman in with his revolutionary march in Krasnoe Selo! Why does Maklakov always let fly on the people at once? Is this never going to end? This damned industrialism. In the country everything is going splendidly; things might stop quiet for centuries to come. If Jaurès hears how many men we shot yesterday, he will turn half the Chamber against us in Paris."

The car draws near the great quays. It is close on midnight, but the bands are still playing in the open-air restaurants. After this hot day the city longs for a breath of air. The Minister's thoughts pass from the Palais Bourbon to the bankers of Paris; he thinks of the conditions imposed with the last two and a half milliards of francs, when France expressly insisted on new strategic railways through Poland. How closely the golden chain of those many, many millions binds the two peoples together! Then he remembers the article Suchomlinov wrote a few weeks ago, haranguing half Europe: *"Russia is prepared; France must prepare, too,"* and urging France to introduce the three years' military service. "The fact is, we need three-quarters of a million French troops besides the two million that we can raise ourselves each winter; without that the risk is too great. It's a good thing we were so sure of Poincaré; in his very first message he announced: *'France must be great and strong in the interests of civilisation and of peace. What we need, first and foremost is energy!'*   A very pretty way of *not* mentioning *revanche!"*

The minister has thought himself into a state of uneasiness. Telegrams from Vienna and Belgrade hint at decisive events. Moreover, he has presentiments. Realist though he is, he has a strain of mysticism in him; and while he weighs plans and sentiments, he calls to the chauffeur: *"No, drive to the Ministry!"* The night-porter is astonished, the servants run forward, doors fly open; only the ciphering department is full of admiration for their chief's *flair*—they are just at work on a long telegram from Belgrade, which will be ready in twenty minutes.

So Viviani was right. We ought to have got in before them. Berchtold has correctly calculated the very hour when our Frenchmen were leaving us.

Sazonov curbs his impatience by signing papers. As he sits at his desk in the night, before the wide-open window, in his full-dress uniform and decorations, his interesting head acquires romantic significance: a bony Russian type, large nose, black eyebrows finely curved, a short, black beard running up in a narrow line under his ears, the corners of his mouth pulled down, somewhat foxy, cold, cruel.

At midnight the deciphered ultimatum from Vienna is brought to him.

*   *

Next morning Europe woke out of its summer siesta with a cry. Cabinets and Embassies, General Staffs and Heads of Banks in every capital became busy, cut their holidays short, recalled their personnel; uneasy, curious, alarmed.

Here in Petersburg most of the great men in the Cabinet and the General Staff are pleasantly excited. They had long hankered for war: *"Serbia's Promised Land lies in the territory of the Austria-Hungary of to-day." "Time is working for Serbia and for the destruction of her enemies, who already show signs of plain dissolution."* These are the words, not of some irresponsible newspaper article, but of the State Despatch in which Sazonov encouraged the hearts of the Belgrade Government after the first Balkan War. In the autumn of 1913 the Frenchman had written home from Petersburg: *"Since the beginning of the Balkan crisis Russia has been seeking above all the humiliation of Austria in the Balkans, as revenge for the humiliation which Count Aehrenthal inflicted on Russia in 1908."* And in January 1914 the Russian Minister of War and the Chief of the General Staff together *"gave a categorical assurance that Russia was fully prepared for a duel with Germany, not to speak of one with Austria."*

To-day at noon, in this same Petersburg, three mighty realms sat at table together. The nimble Frenchman had made sure of the Foreign Minister by telephone, early in the morning, by promising him a dish which no one else could set before him this day: namely, the British Ambassador. At this luncheon, Sir George Buchanan, a Conservative, not perhaps pro-French, but pro-Russian and certainly anti-German, was forced unwillingly into the defensive. Their host, M. Paléologue, was supple, persuasive, and certainly the most excited of the three at this historic meal. Poincaré's conversation during the last few days had brought his emotions to boiling-point. As long as three weeks ago he had prophesied to Briand: *"I am convinced the storm is coming; when and where it will break, I could not say."*

Sazonov, on the contrary, had not yet reached the point of wanting war. Serbia had, after all, put Vienna in a position of moral superiority. Russia herself, despite the soldiers' assurances, was not ready; that he knew for certain. His idea was, therefore, partial mobilisation to keep Germany out of the conflict; pressure on Austria to save

COUNT SERGIUS DEMITRIEWITSCH SAZONOV

Secretary for Foreign Affairs in the Czar's Cabinet

Serbia after Austria had won her opening victories. He knew that the partial mobilisation would hold Roumania in check; if necessary, it could be represented as a measure taken in defence of the Treaty of Bucharest. A diplomatic victory, the Central Powers put in the shade, Aehrenthal's glory of 1909 extinguished. But supposing Germany mobilised, too? Then Russia would be the aggrieved party. France would have a *casus belli* that she could proclaim to all the world; there were no limits to the possibilities which might arise if one could make sure of England. Then the ultimate goal, the Dardanelles, would be within sight!

This same morning his Ambassador to Paris, who had arrived with Poincaré but had stopped on in Petersburg, had expounded this to him with rapier-like energy. It was Isvolski's dream.

At the luncheon table the Frenchman and the Russian exert themselves, for different reasons but with equal passion, to get the Englishman to speak. "If he once declares his hand," thinks the Frenchman, "we shall start this war with assurance of victory!" "If he declares for us before all the world," thinks the Russian, "either the Triple Alliance will draw back, or we shall win!" The Frenchman thinks of war; the Russian, like the Serb, wants to leave two ways open; the bloodless path seems to him on the whole better for the present.

All three agree at table on two points: Vienna is mad and Berlin is behind it. Paléologue's report reproduces the main points of this conversation:

The Frenchman: *"We shall do what is necessary. The Tsar and our President promised each other only yesterday to act firmly and resolutely."*

The Russian: *"But suppose that policy is bound to lead to war?"*

The Frenchman: *"It will lead to war only if the Germanic Powers have already made up their minds to resort to force."*

The Englishman: *"I assume that my Government will desire to remain neutral, and I am therefore apprehensive that France and Russia will be crushed by the Triple Alliance."*

A pause. The host of the house and the host of the country preserve an embarrassed silence. Then Sazonov says in a determined voice: *"At the present juncture England's neutrality would be tantamount to her suicide."*

"Don't you see," cries Paléologue, backing him up, *"that England can play the decisive part here? Only four days ago the Tsar said to me: 'Unless Germany has lost her reason altogether she will never dare to attack Russia, France, and England combined.'"*

This is all very painful to Sir George Buchanan. He says: *"I'm afraid public opinion with us is still far from realising what our national interests so imperiously require. We are not directly interested in Serbia, and the man in the street would never approve a war on her account."*

Thus the three Powers had taken up their positions on the first day.

* *

The Ministerial Council lasted five hours. It adjourned till the Council of State on the next day, but before doing so decided that Vienna must give Belgrade a respite, in order to allow the Powers to study the material brought forward against Serbia; and the Minister of War was instructed, *"in case of necessity"* to order mobilisation against Austria. A public manifesto declared that Russia could not remain indifferent. In the morning the Austrian Ambassador called on the Foreign Minister; in the evening the German. They were very different, and disliked one another strongly.

Count Szapary is a typical, pleasant-mannered Hungarian cavalier; Count Pourtalès a stiff Prussian official, with square-cut head, grizzled beard, thick underlip, a departmental official, short of sight and understanding.

The Hungarian reads the note to Serbia officially, but Sazonov repeatedly interrupts him; he wishes to appear more agitated than he really is, in order that Szapary may report "excitement in Russia" to Vienna. *"You want formal declarations from Pashitch? Il dira cela dix fois, si vous voulez. But Serbia will no longer be master in her own house, after your demands! You will always be wanting to intervene again, and what a life you will lead Europe!"*

The Hungarian reads on.

Sazonov: *"Why has the Cabinet in Vienna given itself all this trouble, when it has already delivered the ultimatum? It is quite a mistake to suppose that the feelings of the Monarchy are shared by all civilised nations."*

"It would be regrettable if we could not come to an understanding with Russia on this question, in which everything which is most sacred to us, and everything which is sacred in Russia, is at stake."

"The monarchical idea has nothing to do with this matter. You want to make war with Serbia, whatever happens!"

"We are the most peace-loving Power in the world, but what we want is security for our territory from foreign revolutionary intrigues and the protection of our dynasty from bombs."

"*Peace-loving? You are setting Europe in flames.*"

These violent exchanges last an hour and a half.

In the evening the German Ambassador declares solemnly that Germany stands unconditionally at Austria's side.

"*Austria-Hungary offered a dossier for investigation when an ultimatum had already been presented. Can you approve of that?*"

"*I regret, Your Excellency, to be unable to discuss that point with you. Austria-Hungary cannot accept interference in her difference with Serbia, and Germany also on her side cannot accept a suggestion which would be contrary to the dignity of her ally as a Great Power.*"

"*We shall not leave Serbia alone in her struggle against Austria.*"

"*You do not like Austria well enough. Why do you want to envenom the last years of a venerable monarch?*"

Sazonov gives the German a hostile look, and answers coldly:

"*No, indeed, we do not like Austria. And why should we like her? She has never done us anything but harm. And if her venerable Monarch has still a crown on his head, he has us to thank for it. Be pleased to remember how he proved his gratitude to*

*us in 1855, 1878, and 1908. Reproach us, indeed,
with not liking Austria!"*

The Minister grows heated, the Ambassador
takes his departure. Immediately afterwards, Sazonov repeats the story to the Frenchman, con-
cluding:

*"The conversation ended in a very acrimonious
tone."*

*   *

The Crown Council was held the next day out
at Krasnoe Selo. This was a fatality. The plain
was gleaming with soldiers, farther than the eye
could reach; the little town clanking with staff
officers, a war-like hum over all. The Tsar, shy and
naturally peaceable, was surrounded at the inspec-
tion by officers only, his Generals, Chiefs-of-Staff,
and Grand Dukes—a threatening circle. On top
of this, as soon as luncheon was over the answer
arrived from Vienna, refusing to prolong the Ultimatum in any circumstances. Feeling had been
serious and moderate before; now it gave way to
fury. All this, combined with the tone of the Note
and the after-effects of Poincaré's provocative attitude, seemed to legitimise the natural desire for
war entertained by the officers.

At the Court table, beside the Tsar, sat the Military Attaché of the German Embassy, General von Chelius, a highly cultivated man who respected the humanist tradition of his name and knew how to seem unaware of the angry looks and words around him. The Governor of Petersburg makes a slip, and speaks of mobilisation in the General's hearing. The Tsar's Equerry turns to him pleasantly and says: *"I cannot tell you what was determined at noon to-day; you can take it from me, however, that the situation is very serious."* Then he clinks glasses with the German and says significantly, as though in farewell: *"Let us hope that we see each other again in better times."*

At six o'clock a General looks at his watch. The time-limit has expired. He says to the German: *"The guns along the Danube have probably already commenced their fire, for one only sends a Note like that after the cannon have been loaded."*

At the opera, that evening, the Tsar receives an ovation, carefully engineered by the Grand Duke Nicholas. The Crown Council had determined the Grand Duke's attitude. Immensely tall, with a grey, pointed beard, a reckless expression, Francophil since happy Paris days, Grand Duke and desperado, a man who (one imagines) might take a whip to his women and his servants, husband of a passionate Montenegrin who has been intriguing against Germany for years—he has long been the brain and fist of the Russian war party against Germany.

His neighbour at to-day's Crown Council was Suchomlinov, the Minister of War, a man of the fat, bluff type, author of the famous article *"Russia is Prepared"* and of the memoranda of recent years on the conquest of the Straits. Beside him, a man of similar views, Yanushkyevitch, Chief of the General Staff; then old Goremykin, the Minister-President, a good fellow, sitting on the fence as always. Sazonov himself does not advocate war; he hopes that the threat implicit in the mobilisation will be enough. The old and dignified Count Fredericks alone, a Baltic aristocrat, the only man at Court who has no enemies, although honours have been pouring on him for years, gives voice to his friendship for Germany at this sitting.

In the President's chair, a pale, weak man, vacant of eye, bowed under the weight of his uniform and decorations—what can this Tsar do against the tiger-glances of his uncle, the Grand Duke, when no peaceable Cabinet, when not even Rasputin, stands by him? Have they not been dinning into the Tsar's ears ever since the Balkan Wars, since Aehrenthal's day and since their defeat by Japan, that only a great war, side by side with

COUNT SUCHOMLINOV
Minister of War for Russia

France, can save the glory and power of the throne? He has hardly begun to point out the difficulties of mobilising during the great strike, when Maklakov rises in his chair, opposite.

This is, perhaps, the most powerful, certainly the most striking, figure at the table. His brow is the highest, his eye the most piercing, and even a thin beard does little to mitigate the weight of this Roman head: a fighter who can wait, but when he strikes, strikes home. Formerly the Government used to fear his species; now that he is Minister of the Interior, the Tsar fears him; for his great hand points to the street when danger threatens, his word seems to set revolution humming before it breaks out. A little while ago he was playing "panther" with the Imperial children; but when he leaped off the chair, the Tsaritsa was more frightened than the children.

Now he stands up and shows that the only way left of averting the internal danger is by a national appeal to arms. War, as escape from the foe within. Resolved: to consider mobilising thirteen corps against Austria, but to make the execution dependent on the attack on Serbia; the date, on the Foreign Minister.

CHAPTER VI

AT SEA

THE *France* rushed onward through the night. It was the very hour in which the Serbian and Russian Premiers were driving to their capitals to face the decisions forced on them by the action of the War Counts in Vienna. And as the thoughts of both men turned to the past, as they used the last hours of leisure to remember and compare, even so was it with these leaders on board, who had been waiting and listening for years for the sound of strife in Europe.

Poincaré had been living through his supreme moment. It was surely even greater than the moment when, just after his election, he showed himself on the balcony of the Elysées, while the Parisians, mocking as ever, shouted his name in a jest— Poing carré. Were not the dreams of his youth surpassed, now, when seated on the left hand of the marble-pale Tsáritsa he drove between the files of the Imperial Guard, while the Tsar rode beside the resplendent carriage? Hardly in his most optimistic moments had the silent ambitions of the lawyer of thirty years ago risen to such heights. Now life called for the supreme effort to reap the full harvest of decades of passionate determination. To drive his people into war was impossible, and well he knew it; but if the hereditary enemy, in a heedless moment, offered an opening and began first, or if one could only make it seem so—what a wondrous destiny to be leader of the French in such an hour! In this hour Poincaré might have been compared to a maiden longing in a dream for the ecstasy of enravishment.

In other respects, indeed, he was not precisely innocent. For he was one of the few men in power who fostered in their own bosoms the flame of *revanche,* fast dying out in the French people. No wonder; he was from Lorraine, and after the war he confessed: *"During my school years"* (immediately after the war of 1870) *"my spirit, oppressed by the defeat, unceasingly crossed the frontier which the Treaty of Frankfurt had imposed on us, and when I climbed down from my castles in the air, I saw no reason for existence for my generation but the hope of recovering the lost provinces."*

This event had coloured all his youth; he could

never forget it, and hence it was that after the war one of his friends could praise him *"for the admirable continuity of his actions."*

The continuity was not uninterrupted, for the revengeful boy grew into a statesman who had learnt how to wait. In the Bosnian crisis he had categorically declared to his allies that France would never let herself be dragged into a war for Russian interests in the Balkans. In August 1912 he had actually warned Sazonov: *"Do not count on our military assistance in the Balkans, even if you are attacked by Austria."* Soon afterwards, however, in November 1912, he turned the decisive corner; and to the great joy of Isvolski (whom, incidentally, he cordially disliked) he adopted an *"entirely new point of view."* *"Territorial gains by Austria would jeopardise the general equilibrium, and would so jeopardise France's own interests";* in this way France might be *"drawn into military operation."* (The cowardly paraphrase adopted by all the diplomats of Europe to avoid the ominous word "war," just as one speaks of "a growth," and not of "cancer.") In January 1914, Poincaré had even assured the Russians through Delcassé *"in the name of the French Foreign Minister, that France will go as far as Russia may wish."* This all-important blank cheque

which Paris now gave to Petersburg, after refusing it two years previously, was limited indeed to
a special case (Liman von Sanders in Constantinople); but for all that it had a psychological effect similar to that of the corresponding concession
given by the Kaiser to Vienna, again after refusing
it two years previously. The same month the President had said to Judet: *"Russia has an enormous
future, her power is in full development. . . . In
two years there will be war. All my efforts will be
directed towards setting us in readiness."*

Poincaré walks to and fro on deck, thinking of
the last hour of ceremony when the Tsar, his guest
here on board, exchanged toasts with him, paced
up and down at his side, and applauded each sug-
gestive phrase as it fell from him. Would their
effect be lasting? The Tsar had seen through him
clearly enough, for soon afterwards he told his
Danish cousins: *"In any case, M. Poincaré does
not want peace for its own sake, as I do. He believes in a successful war."*

Probably in this hour the President once more
reviews the recent epoch. Is it really only five
weeks since he formed a cabinet with his nervous
associate Viviani? Elections for the Chamber in
April, then the infernal second ballots, ending in
the victory of the Socialists in May, a few more

opponents of the three years' military service enter-
ing the Chamber at the last moment.   Paléologue
claimed the victory for himself; he said that he
had convinced the President.

And what may Viviani be thinking of during
these hours on board the *France?* More emotional
and more cynical than Poincaré, and also less pe-
dantic, he seems to be the right Chief of Staff for
the other's Field-Marshal attitude. Is he not
quietly enjoying the joke of Paléologue's excitement over social details; his fetching Lemaître
specially from Paris to arrange the flowers for
the dinner in the Embassy? It is true that afterwards his Ambassador had given him some important hints of how feeling was running. At the
revue in the Grand Duke's tent the two Montene-
grins, Anastasia and Militza, had chattered to him:
*"Don't you realise that we are passing through
historical days, fateful days! I've had a telegram
from my father to-day. He tells me we shall have
war before the end of the month! What a hero
my father is! He's worthy of the Iliad! Just look
at this little box I always take about with me.. It
has some Lorraine soil in it, real Lorraine soil I
scraped up on the frontier when I was in France
with my husband, two years ago. Look there, at
the table of honour: it's covered with thistles. I*

gathered several plants on the annexed terri-
tory, brought them here and had the seeds sown in
my garden. You'll see. There'll be nothing left
of Austria. You're going to get back Alsace and
Lorraine. Our armies will meet in Berlin." Then
suddenly, breaking off: *"I must restrain myself.*
The Tsar has his eye on me."

Thus the two Frenchmen, cleverer than their colleagues in Berlin, but in no way less ready for
war; held more firmly in check by the machinery
of a Republic, but up to every trick of deceiving
the people; thus they recall the lowering atmosphere of those festal days, weigh the words of
hysterical Grand Duchesses as they will appear
later in their memoirs. They are like spectators at
a play, imagining during the interval what the next
act will be like, and hoping that it will go thus
and not otherwise.

Then a sailor runs up the companionway and
hands over a long wireless message; it is Vienna's
Ultimatum to Serbia, sent on. Salvation! Poincaré orders the homeward route to be shortened,
Viviani begins to send instructions to Paris. Full
steam for home!

*   *

When next the sun sets behind the heights of
Malmö, the chiefs of two States stand on the

bridges of their respective ships and look round, get their officers to look, calculate, and look again. Each of them might easily reckon that the threatened complications in Europe were calling the other home, so that their courses might quite possibly cross each other. At the same hour the *France* was bearing her President through the North Sea to Dunkirk, and the *Hohenzollern* was carrying the Kaiser to Kiel. Each heart was beating in anticipation of war, each knew that the air around him was quivering with the electric waves, above in their cabins their wireless officers heard the stammer of speech in foreign tongues—but, alas! all was safely enciphered. Nevertheless, on board the hostile ships they made some attempts at deciphering; then they gave it up.

The two rulers on their ships weighed the course of destiny of these days. The Frenchman was torn between contradictory feelings; he admits himself that he wanted *revanche;* consequently he was bound to hope that war would be forced on him; yet he could not but fear the devastation bound to fall on his own homeland, Lorraine, and, as he was not in a position to attack, he must prefer that any German plans should be postponed until 1917. And yet he had spoken plainly enough, the last time only yesterday, to the Tsar. The Kaiser's

RAYMOND POINCARÉ
Prime Minister of France, 1914–

feelings were swayed, as was inevitable with a
vacillating nature such as his, by moods and circumstances; surrounded for weeks at a time only
by soldiers and other persons who had studied him
for years past, and had been freshly oiled, like
the ship's engines, before starting, by their instigators in Berlin; breathing the atmosphere of "an
Admiral of the Atlantic Ocean," and hearing not
a single outspoken word of political warning; even
more entirely out of touch with all classes of the
people than when at home; and, to crown all,
honestly infuriated by the murder of his friend—
what could he think but what the following notes
show, written in his own hand on board the *Hohenzollern* during his July trip, on the margin of the
latest despatches:

Report from Vienna in which the Ambassador
speaks of Berchtold's endeavours to find demands
that it would be wholly impossible for Serbia to
accept. Note by the Kaiser: *"Evacuate the Sandjak! Then the row would be on at once! Austria
must absolutely get that back, in order to prevent
the Serbs from gaining the sea-coast!"*

Tisza wanted them to act *"like gentlemen,"*
thereby interfering with Berchtold's plans. Note
by the Kaiser: *"To murderers, after what has happened! Rubbish! . . . It was like this at the time of*

the Silesian wars: 'I am against all councils of War and conferences, since the more timid party always has the upper hand. Frederick the Great.'"

Report from London that the Government "*expects that Berlin has succeeded in suppressing demands by Vienna which cannot be met.*" Note by the Kaiser: "*Why should I do any such thing? None of my business! What does 'cannot be met' mean? The rascals have added murder to agitation and must be punished.*" "*London hopes that Vienna will not insist on demands that are plainly intended to bring on war.*" Note by the Kaiser: "*That is a tremendous piece of British insolence! I am not called upon to prescribe à la Grey to H. M. the Emperor how to preserve his honour!*"

Jagow agrees that London should be told that we have no influence over these internal affairs. Note by the Kaiser: "*Grey must be told this plainly and seriously! So that he will see that I am not in the mood for joking. . . . Serbia is a band of robbers that must be seized for its crimes . . . The real British reasoning and condescending way of giving orders, which I insist on having rebuffed. Wilhelm. I.R.*"

Reports from Vienna that Berchtold has given the Russians a complete assurance that Austria wants no aggrandisement at Serbia's expense.

Note by the Kaiser: *"Ass! She must take back the Sandjak, else the Serbs will reach the Adriatic."*

Report from London on Grey's first idea of a Conference. Note by the Kaiser: *"I will not join in, unless Austria expressly asks me to, which is not likely. In questions of honour and vital interests one does not consult with others."*

A report from Petersburg on Sazonov's threat that if Austria devours Serbia he will go to war. Note by the Kaiser: *"Well, go to it."*

Report from Rome, with a warning about Italy's attitude. Note by the Kaiser: *"This is all bosh, and it will come out all right in the end itself."*

Bethmann reports that he thinks German's attitude should remain calm for the moment. Note by the Kaiser: *"Calmness is the first duty of a citizen! Keep calm—only keep calm!!! But a calm mobilisation is something new indeed."*

In this mood the Kaiser arrived at Potsdam.

CHAPTER VII

HESITATIONS

ENGLAND was agitated. What spirit of war had entered into this calm nation, whose common sense made her pacifist, whose geographical situation made her neutral, whose national tradition made her cautious? For weeks past the streets and the Press had been full of talk of volunteers, guns, munitions, even before those thoughts and terms became popular on the Continent itself. What had happened to break the repose of these islands?

One of them, Ireland, had rebelled against the other, and when the Liberal Cabinet tried to pacify her with fresh liberties, a province of that same island cut itself loose from the rest and threatened by force of arms the introduction of freedom. The Protestants of Ulster protested. They would not remain alone on their island with their hated southern brothers; they would rather die as

English old maids than contract a marriage of convenience with their neighbors. They proposed to defend their virginity with barricades and muskets; but it was only when their brothers of the south became active that the importation of arms to Ireland was forbidden and the coast searched for mines and guns. The government felt itself freed from its pledge of Home Rule by the Ulster rebellion, but at the same time the unrest in the South was alarming. What is to be done? debated the King with his Ministers. Shall we treat the world to the spectacle of civil war in Great Britain?

While they were still deliberating, a fresh alarm ran through cities and streets. The Curragh, an old and important military training-centre, rebelled against the War Office in London. High officers refused obedience to the Government and proposed to overturn it for being in their eyes too lenient altogether towards the Irish. For many generations England had been ruled by common sense and majorities; by imagination and adventure too, but by the sword hardly ever. Now storms were gathering, over yonder on the unrestful island and in England itself; Parliament, from which the Government was drawn, seemed endangered by a few officers and a corps of volunteers. People did not trust their eyes or ears. In the middle of England

one might have thought oneself in Zabern. Asquith saved himself and the Cabinet by suddenly
taking over the War Office himself.

In this din the shots from Sarajevo were lost.
What have we to do with Serbia? asked the man
in the street, turning over the page of his paper
and looking for the latest telegram from Belfast
and the Curragh. Only a few knew what struggles
were meanwhile shaking the Cabinet; no one saw
the struggle in the souls of the leaders.

The Government was strangely enough com-
pounded. In essence it consisted of five men, while
two others made themselves important by leading
an opposition. Of the rest of the crew, three were
ballast and two able seamen.

Asquith, with the head of a Dickens character
and the nature of a Roman, regards the world with
intelligent eyes; and when he speaks, his beardless
mouth gives sharp expression to the passionless
thoughts which he accompanies with the sparing
gestures of an Englishman. Always calm, sometimes hesitating, a realist, but with a certain fear
of quick decisions, he is leader of the House rather
than of the Cabinet. He is for "peace with
honour," and at first looks at the conflict very
much from a distance. At the Peace Congress six
years earlier he had said: "The vast armaments are

not being accumulated for ornament or for amusement, but for use when the time comes; perhaps in a mere chance outburst of ill-temper."

Lord Haldane is less at his ease; a humanist with the head of an old cardinal by Tintoretto, with a brooding nature lit by sudden flashes. He has a weakness for Germany; for that reason he has a better understanding of Germany's weaknesses. He knew Goethe. He had studied philosophy in Göttingen and planned a technical college for London on the Berlin model; then King Edward's faith in him put him at the head of the War Office to enlarge England's small army and remodel the General Staff on German lines. Thus destiny chose him to forge arms against the country that he loved. This seemed but to strengthen his determination not to use his arms except in case of necessity, and two years previously he had returned from Berlin in some dejection, having vainly offered an agreement on the scale and rate of naval construction, which was frustrated by Tirpitz. In these negotiations, which were made more difficult for him by the lack of harmony between Emperor, Chancellor, and High Admiral, he had been disappointed, not so much by the demands as by the men. He had offered understanding and found mistrust. Was it not in-

evitable that he should grow daily more unhappy
through this month of July?

Paler still grew his friend Sir Edward Grey,
the Foreign Minister, who for eight years past had
been keeping not only England, but the whole
Continent from plunging into war. His was the
strangest character of all the five. In him were
mingled an Englishman's fears for his country,
whose situation, dependent as it was for 80 per
cent. of its food supply on imports, any war must
endanger, with a European outlook and a Christian
wish to maintain a pacifist attitude (which no
statesman in Europe could afford at that time,
and which his own policy, despite every good intention, was destined gravely to endanger).

A recluse by nature, seldom seen in society, de-
prived of his wife and his brother by terrible ac-
cidents; a lover of birds, a keen fisherman (and
consequently a man of patience and foresight).
His intellectual features, large, deep-set eyes, thin,
silent mouth, revealed no traces of pretentious-
ness or ambition. He spent his week-ends simply in
the woods, and verses of Wadsworth came more
readily to his lips than Parliamentary speeches.
He is no traveller, speaks no foreign language,
breeds squirrels in the country, loves children, says
little. When, however, he does get up in the House

HON. HERBERT ASQUITH

Prime Minister of Great Britain, 1914–1917

of Commons, all are attentive, for he speaks in
an admirable style, without regard to the Gallery,
and expresses modern ideas in the manner of an
old English aristocrat.

For all that, he was not strong enough, with
Europe in full anarchy, to keep clear of the net-
work of alliances. He sailed too far from the
coast, and in the end his ship was caught in the
storm. Even he fell a victim to the great mistrust
of all for all, and under the threat of the German
naval expansion, after Berlin had refused Haldane's suggestions, he went so far as to extend the
old verbal understanding between King Edward
and France into an agreement which provided that
in certain circumstances, in case of an attack by
a third party, England consented to undertake the
protection of the north coast of France. The single
document in which he involved his country in the
possibility of war was a letter to the French Ambassador, Cambon, in which he promised, in case
France were seriously threatened, to negotiate on
the question of common action.

But this decisive letter, which was known to the
Cabinet, had compromised England's freedom more
than the words said. Grey himself believed he had
a "free hand"; in reality he had imposed a moral
obligation on England. The official consultations,

and still more the private fraternisations between
the Admiralties and General Staffs, had created
an atmosphere which was bound gradually to stifle
the free breath of the Foreign Minister. An able
English historian, Dr. Gooch, speaks of *"de facto
obligations,"* even where none exist in writing;
Lloyd George of an *"obligation of honour,"*
Churchill actually of a position in which England
had *"the obligations of an alliance without its ad-
vantages. . . . We were morally bound to come to
the aid of France."*

When the King and Queen visited Paris in the
April of 1914 and Grey imbibed a whiff of Continental atmosphere, he avoided assuming fresh obligations, but did not prevent the Admiralty
from arranging with Russia that England—still
only in case of attack—should *"hold"* a portion of
the German fleet for Russia *"in the North Sea."*
While he spoke and dreamt of peace and understanding, he could not prevent the officers of the
General Staff, Sir Henry Wilson at their head,
from drilling into their subordinates the idea of
war, and of war against Germany; nor could he
prevent the plans for the landing of the six di-
visions from being worked out to the last detail.
Moreover, the intimacy between the three War
Offices and Admiralties kept growing steadily. The

Russian Ambassador was able to write home from London in the summer of 1914: *"I doubt whether any better guarantee for joint military operations in the event of war could be found than the spirit of this Entente as it now reveals itself, strengthened by the existing military agreements."* Grey and his Government now had no other way out but to *"turn a blind eye to the facts,"* to wash their hands in ignorance, and (as his Conservative opponents maintained) to sit on the fence and try to remain friends with everybody.

So it was that when questioned in the House in the spring of 1914 he avoided affirming the existence of an agreement with Russia. He defended himself afterwards in these words: *"Parliament has an unqualified right to know of any agreement or arrangements that bind the country to action or restrain its freedom. But it cannot be told of military or naval measures to meet possible contingencies. Political engagements ought not to be kept secret; naval or military preparations for contingencies of war are necessary but must be kept secret. In these instances care had been taken to ensure that such preparations did not involve any political engagement."* This was, technically speaking, true, and only proves once more the complete defencelessness of every country in Europe, the fear which dominated every Minister, and their readiness to take refuge behind the cannon; for thither the general European anarchy was forcing them.

The dominating factors in this nation of shopkeepers, that could never wish for the destruction of its largest customer, forced it, despite increasing competition, into a position which resembled in general that between Sparta and Athens. "We shall never consent to the destruction of Athens," Sparta had said in reply to representations from Thebes, "for Greece without Athens would be but a man with one eye." The growing population and growing unrest of the German people, its police spirit, and above all the glitter of its "shining sword," made Kaiser and Empire unpopular in Great Britain; but there was never a word or even a thought of a planned attack.

For all that, Grey knew how easily, in the disingenuous and undeveloped state of international law, any party could manufacture an alleged "violation of the frontier," and so accuse any other of that aggression which itself was undertaking or wished to undertake.

Lloyd George was the Celt in the Cabinet, and consequently something of a poet; besides this, being the son of a poor schoolmaster, he knew the

people. Adroit and popular, eloquent and energetic, he commanded a variety of talents which
gradually carried him into a position for which
he was in some respects too strong. He was as
wholly a man of practical experience as Asquith of
legal theory. He was as demagogic and fond of
applause as Grey was deliberate, peace-loving, and
solitary. He thought best with his eyes, and if he
wished to understand some point concerning a ship
or a mine, would go down into the pit or out to sea,
and look. He had studied the German method of
dealing with social questions, but unfamiliar as
he was with the arts and sciences, he remained a
stranger to the best side of the German people, and
disliked it as much as he did the French. Nevertheless, his vision was clear, and, six years before, he
had told his countrymen openly that Germany's
activities were perfectly comprehensible; that they
themselves would lay in stores of ships and guns,
if they had to face the possibility of a European
war with the enemy on either flank. Time and
again he had condemned the armaments race as
senseless. Of all the Cabinet, he was certainly the
least of a man of the world, and also the least of a
typical Englishman.

The last of the five was both of these. Churchill,
a descendant of the Duke of Marlborough, half

American by blood and a man of worldwide experience, was certainly bent on strengthening the country which had helped him to power and position. Neither meditative like Grey nor placid like Asquith, neither a deep thinker like Haldane nor a man of the people like Lloyd George, though an extremely talented writer and historian, he had knocked about for a decade or two, partly for adventure's sake, sampling wars and continents, shining in the arts and sciences, writing brilliant books about military administration and free trade, which were always, also, books about Churchill; always fertile of imagination, always keen of eye and swift of foot. He had done much to further the British naval expansion. Swashbuckler that he was, he knew what war was like; he and Enver Pasha were probably the only Ministers in Europe at that time who had had personal experience of soldiering at the front.

Of the five important Cabinets in Europe, the British, which was practically controlled by these five men, was the least anxious for war, opposed it longest, and yet failed to stop it, although it was precisely this Cabinet, and now only this Cabinet, that could have succeeded.

*   *

For eighteen months past a new German Ambassador had been earning praise in London, jealousy in Berlin. Prince Lichnowsky, who was as friendly to the country to which he was accredited as to his own fatherland, had always warned his Government of the consequences of the German naval programme against England, and Germany's attachment to Austria. If to be fonder of England than of Austria was a mistake, it was a mistake only because he had failed, or so long as he failed, to reach a position strong enough to enable him to reconstruct German policy single-handed. His rank, his wealth, and his relations with the Kaiser, who treated him as an intimate friend and received private reports from him, made him more independent than his colleagues. Standing outside, he tried to turn the central wheels of policy, thereby multiplying his enemies in the Foreign Office and making it difficult for his friends to work for him. He was looked on as a dilettante, because he was neither a Prussian official with all the limitations and virtues of the type, nor the real working leader of a mission, but rather confined himself to using his personal influence, for he had ideas of his own. He knew the historical forces which had made England strong and Austria weak, and his personal experience seemed to con-

firm his views; for although he owned estates in
Austria, the family had been disliked there since
his father's days, while his attitude and habits
made him popular in London.

Lichnowsky was the first man to bring the tone
of a Continental European into the debate between Vienna and Berlin. He wrote at once to
Berlin that *"to brand the entire Serbian nation as
a race of rascals and murderers . . . presents difficulties. . . . Austria's policy must be considered as
mere adventure, inasmuch as it will lead neither to
a radical solution of the problem nor to the annihilation of the Greater Serbia movement."* Up till
shortly before the Ultimatum he issued repeated
warnings against supporting the Balkan adventure. *"Finally, as far as the localisation of the
struggle is concerned, you must admit that such a
localisation, in the event of a passage at arms with
Serbia, belongs in the realms of pious wishes. Consequently, to my mind everything seems to depend
on whether the Austrian demands can be so formulated that, with the help of some pressure from
Petersburg and London, they can be accepted in
Belgrade; not, however, so formulated that they
will of necessity lead to a war ad majorem illustris-
simi comitis de Berchtold gloriam."* These warnings, which were followed in the next

week by many similar ones, give him an honourable
place in the eyes of history amongst the three German diplomats who saw rightly at that time.

Jagow, who also had long since ceased to believe
in the Austrian fetish, but went on worshipping it,
quoted Wilhelm Busch against Lichnowsky:

> "*If you're tired of present company,*
> *Look for another, if such there be.*"

Austria, he argued, was weakened by Balkan
crises and had almost ceased to be a Great Power,
and for that very reason we must support her. "*To
be sure, there will be some agitation in Petersburg,
but on the whole Russia is not ready to strike at
present. Nor will France or England be anxious
for war at the present time. . . . Our group, meanwhile, is becoming steadily weaker. . . . If we cannot attain localisation and if Russia attacks Austria
. . . we could not throw Austria over then. . . . I
desire no preventive war, but if war should come,
we cannot hide behind the fence.*"

This letter, particularly its close, shows how
even the more intelligent in these circles never
quite overcome the effects of their education in the
students' corps and officers' mess.

At the beginning of the crisis all the diplomats
of Europe are praised for their virile attitude.

Berchtold is even said to be *"in very good spirits,"* whereas as early as the beginning of July foreign diplomats mention Lichnowsky's *"worried expression,"* which speaks well for him. The fact that, in spite of entirely different habits and interests, he gets on admirably with Grey speaks well for them both. The two had just combined to solve two difficult questions in Asia Minor and Portuguese Africa, after years of negotiations; and they were, therefore, now able to be more open with each other than any other corresponding pair. Grey gives the Ambassador a direct answer to a direct question: England has no definite treaties, but her relations with France and Russia are *"very intimate."*

Grey's whole nature could not but revolt against Serbia; blood and scandal had marked this dynasty's chequered history. Grey remembers the murder of Prince Michael, the abduction of the Crown Prince, Milan's abdication, Alexander's misalliance, the murder of Alexander and his wife, the scandals about the Crown Prince George. Nevertheless, his first comment on the Ultimatum, on July 24th, was that he *"had never before seen one State address to another independent State a document of so formidable a character."*

That was what he said to Mensdorff, the Austrian Ambassador, a sensible Austrian Count.

Mensdorff, Lichnowsky, and the Russian Ambassador, Count Benckendorff, are all related to
one another, and under the pressure of their mis-
sions will soon become enemies, just as the three
sovereigns used their relationship to crush the
brotherhood which linked their peoples. And now,
in the whole spider's web of *démarches,* notes, con-
ventions, and alliances, Grey—first of any man in
Europe—does the natural thing: he speaks to
Lichnowsky of the horrors of a war between four
nations. *"However the affair might come out, one
thing is certain: that is total exhaustion and im-
poverishment. Industry and trade will be ruined,
and the power of capital destroyed. Revolutionary movements like those of the year 1848, due to
the collapse of industrial activity, will be the result."*

On these first two days Grey, now much alarmed
by the rumours of Petersburg's decision, speaks
in three directions. To the Serbs through a representative, advising them to reply favourably so far
as possible, but also to ask the opinion of the representatives of the other Powers in Belgrade; to the
Austrians, urging them to do everything that could
be done to avert the danger which threatened. To
the Germans he said: *"I fully recognise the justice
of the Austrian demand for satisfaction, as well as*

*the desire for the punishment of all persons con-
nected with the murder. . . . I count with certainty
on the Austrian mobilisation being followed by
that of Russia. Upon that, in my opinion, the
moment will have arrived at which to begin medi-
ating between Russia and Austria in conjunction
with yourselves, France, and Italy. Without your
co-operation all attempts at mediation will be
futile."*

A typical example of international mediation; a
proof that this Englishman at least set the peace
of Europe higher than the system of alliances and
balance of power.

Both Ambassadors telegraph to their Foreign
Offices, but Lichnowsky with true prophetic inspi-
ration adds the words: *"Grey's proposal is the
only possibility of avoiding a world war, in which
for us there would be everything to lose and nothing to gain. . . . In case France should be drawn
in, England would not dare to remain disinter-
ested."*

At the same time Grey sends his third appeal to
Petersburg: *"Public opinion here would not sanc-
tion our going to war over a Serbian quarrel. If,
however, war does take place, the development of
other issues may draw us into it, and I am therefore
anxious to prevent it. . . . The only chance of*

peace, in my opinion, is for the other four Powers
to join in asking the Austrian and Russian Gov-
ernments not to cross the frontier. . . . If Ger-
many will adopt this view, I feel strongly that
France and ourselves should act upon it."

Thus on the same day the German reported to
his Foreign Office as a supposition what England
was reporting to her Embassies both at Berlin and
Petersburg as a possibility: in case of war she
could scarcely remain neutral.

Here the tragic chain of cause and effect begins.
From this moment Grey revolves in his head one
single thought: "Shall I tell the world—shall I
tell Germany, openly, what I am telling my Ambassadors confidentially; that Germany must give
way, because on the outbreak of war we, too, shall
mobilise? Paris and Petersburg are waiting for
our supporting assurance. I cannot give it, for only
Parliament can decide the vital question. If I bind
my country by a 'yes' to-day, that country can dis-
avow me to-morrow, for neither I nor Asquith nor
anyone else knows what the man in the street, what
Press and Parliament will say when it comes to
the point. Everything will then depend on the
circumstances, on whether it looks as though we or
the others were being the aggressors." . . . "And
yet I ought to threaten," his thoughts run on. "In

Berlin and Vienna the soldiers are working for war, and Germany's terrible army, which is better prepared than that of its enemies, can hope for victory over two allies, but not over three."

Grey afterwards described the central point of these inward struggles in these words:

"One danger I saw, so hideous that it must be avoided and guarded against at every word. It was that France and Russia might face the ordeal of war with Germany relying upon our support; that this support might not be forthcoming, and that we might then, when it was too late, be held responsible by them for having let them in for a disastrous war."

Here is revealed, as in a classical tragedy, the desperate situation of a man in authority seeking with all the force of his heart and soul to avoid the false step whose fatal consequences he foresees; and yet fatally doomed, whichever way he turns, to take that false step because, in a weak moment, he had been led into making half-promises. Small is the guilt, pure the will, great the confusion, true the effort, tragic the end.

CHAPTER VIII

EXPECTATION

I N burning anxiety a man is sitting in the express train. Three days, three nights he sits there alone, thinking feverishly; Isvolski's brain is the most tortured in Europe, his heart the most violently moved during these days. There is something symbolic about his dash, just at this moment, from Petersburg to Paris, through the heart of Germany. He is like the angel of terror. Desired so long, felt so near, and now—too soon! Because his whole nature yearned for this war, he had always warned against premature outbreak; he had warned his Minister against Hartwig's intrigues in Belgrade. Not before 1917, and then only if a good start can be ensured! Time cannot but bring Austria to decay—Austria that he so hated; then Isvolski's hour would come. But today? Will Paris dare too much, or too little? Betrayed, perhaps by a few years, certainly by a few hours! If only the telegram from Belgrade had arrived in Petersburg two hours earlier, he would have sailed with the President on board the *France,* which had brought him from Paris. No one would have sought to keep him here, where his pupils and even his enemies can well take his place; he would have passed these vital days of his life, hours fruitful as none other could ever be, at the President's side. Then he and the two leaders of France could together have thought out every move on the chessboard; they could have tested, tried, and agreed on every common step in the quiet of the isolated ship!

At the Warsaw station Paléologue had sworn that the moment had come. *"Cette fois c'est la guerre,"* he had said softly. Yet Paléologue had not the personal motive of revenge—revenge! That was the heartfelt cry which for five years past had rung ceaselessly in Isvolski's brain.

The man looks like a Pasha; one imagines him a master of serfs; powerful head, brutal chin, thick lips, which know how to suck his prey dry; the whole picture brings to mind legends out of darkest Russia, the knout, vodka, and women. But it is all wrapped in a wish, the wish for revenge.

Six years ago now he was sitting in Buchlau, in a castle in Moravia, opposite his Austrian host— sitting in a tall chair at Count Berchtold's hearth.

ISVOLSKI
Member of the Czar's Cabinet

The candles were lit, the coffee was served, the
servants had retired, the doors were shut; then and
there he let Count Aehrenthal dupe him. Surely
Gortchakoff's shadow flitted through the chamber?
Thirty years earlier Gortchakoff had made a secret
pact with Austria: if Austria ever wished to take
and keep the two Turkish provinces, Bosnia and
Herzegovina, which had been given her to ad-
minister, Russia would make no protest; in return,
Austria would stand aside if Russia revised the
Straits Treaty. In Buchlau the moment had come
to fulfil this old agreement, whose authors were
long since skeletons, mouldering in their ancestral
vaults.

And yet at this hearth he let the Austrian dupe
him. Unable to defend himself against the questions in the Duma, he had to go.

Revenge for Buchlau! From that moment the
thought had dominated him. Berchtold, his host
at that meeting, and the pupil of his old enemy—
Berchtold, whom he had disliked even in Petersburg, had since become Foreign Minister in
Vienna. To strike him down, to destroy Austria,
when the moment is ripe, has become the motive of
all his actions. And he intrigues with the Serbians,
incites Tittoni to a campaign against Tripolis, the
Balkans to a war against Stamboul—which means

against Austria—eggs on Roumania; becomes Ambassador in Paris in order the better to whisper into France's ear. With Caillaux, the coward and Germanophile, there is nothing to be done. But after him comes Poincaré; lukewarm M. Louis has to leave Petersburg; every post is filled with friends of the Tsar; Poincaré goes to the Elysée, his influence, instead of sinking, rises steadily; he captivates the Tsar in Paris, and when Isvolski shows him his latest work, the Serbo-Bulgarian secret treaty against the Turks, Poincaré cries out, before he has read it to the end: *"That is the instrument of war!"* Then he says to the Russian: *"If the conflict entails armed intervention by Germany . . . we shall not hesitate one minute to fulfil our obligations towards Russia."* He insists, it is true, that Germany must first have taken the offensive.

Since Agadir, and again since the conversations between the two allies, France's slumbering thoughts of *revanche* had awakened; the visit of the English King had put the finishing touch. Those who were working for war were still only a few dozen or a few hundred men—here as in every corner of Europe—but their voices were loud, their positions powerful, the baits which they offered were tempting. So the Russian Count Benckendorff wrote to Petersburg in February 1913: *"When I sum up Cambon's interviews with me our conversations together, and Poincaré's attitude, I have a feeling which amounts to conviction that of all the Powers, France is the only one which —I will not say wishes for war, but would see it come without much regret."* Poincaré dined with the German Ambassador, the first President to do so since 1870, but his resentful heart beat so loud under the purple ribbon that even Freiherr von Schön heard it. He was only an official, and they dared speak openly with him. Barthou said to him flatly: *"Give us back Alsace and Lorraine, and we shall be the best friends in the world!"* That year they reckoned on the war; General Michel, the Governor of Paris, asked in the budgetary commission for extraordinary provisions of flour for the capital on the grounds that *"this is no ordinary year; we do not know whether we shall not be mobilising in March or April."*

In May the Belgian Minister reported that France had undoubtedly become more chauvinistic: *"they say they are certain of victory."* At the same time, an old diplomat said to him: *"If an awkward incident arises now, the men at the head of the two States will have to agree within three days, or there will be war!"* At the end of May there was ill-feeling because actors appeared on the Berlin stage in the uniform of the Foreign Legion; at the same time Germans were represented in Paris in the villains' parts. At the national celebrations, for the first time, coloured troops appeared in the review.

For two days past Ministry and Press have been raging over the Ultimatum to Serbia, particularly on account of the ruthless time-limit. No one believes Germany's assurance of ignorance; they think that she is making the running for Vienna. French securities sink lower than they have been since 1870, the Bourse has to be shut, the whole world believes that Germany wants war. In the Ministry sits old M. Bienvenu-Martin, representing the two Presidents, both on the ocean. He sends out a ceaseless stream of wireless messages to sea; but in his own activity he lacks talent and brilliancy. So, to begin with, he negotiates regarding Grey's proposal of yesterday for a Conference. He speaks with the German Ambassador: *"Your appeal to us for a united effort for the maintenance of peace,"* says M. Bienvenu, *"has had a very beneficial effect here."*

"Germany is one with France in her warm desire for peace," says Freiherr von Schön. *"It is on Petersburg that the pressure must be brought."*

"I for my part would gladly be willing to have pacifying influences set to work at Petersburg, after it has been established in advance through Austrian assurances that no annexation is contemplated."

"Possible general representations of the Powers at Vienna would not appear to be conformable to our view that Austria-Hungary and Serbia ought to be left alone."

"Lies, lies again, and still they lie," till the air of the room reeks with lies. Not for nothing do they bear their names. [1] The Kaiser is right, when on the same day he writes against the last paragraph of the report—although his remark is, indeed, directed against the Frenchmen only: *"Rubbish clad in stately phrases!"*

[1] Bienvenu = welcome (French). Schön = beautiful (German).— TRANSLATOR'S NOTE.

CHAPTER IX

PROTEST

WHITHER had Reason fled? After hovering here and there, wistful and unregarded, behind the diplomats' armchairs, had she left Europe altogether? Had this furtive spinning of preparations reduced her to utter despair? Padded double doors closing with muffled sound, diplomatic hands which meet and part hastily, the rustle of code-books, the chirp of telephones, the rolling and unrolling of staff maps, the false smiles of all these lords and kings? Was she weary of the silent destroyers, at work behind the closed doors of old palaces on little infernal machines which they will set off punctually at the destined hour to overwhelm the Continent with thunderous destruction? Hopeless, Reason has left the Cabinets and gone into the streets.

The cities are in uproar. Reason has mingled among the millions, now that the twenty or thirty men who were Europe's lords have forsaken them;

among the nameless, now that the great lords with the long names have betrayed them. Now she stings the slaves to protest. They are ready, they need no persuasion. Sullen and sweating, they mutter; behind the lathes and benches, the boilers and steam-hammers, the engines and rollers, they listen to the news the papers bring them of threatening tempest.

But in the evening they stroll out of the grey tenements, the airless, narrow slums, into the brilliant quarters of the rich; here a group of friends, there a man with his wife—and without plan or purpose, thousands of other strollers like themselves meet at the busy street corners where, as the glass doors of the cafés swing to and fro, the sound of music mingles with the roar of the street without. There they meet, weary but excited; strangers to one another and yet familiar; the same clothes, the same expressions, the same pale faces show the growing thought that obsesses them all.

Among them are a few young fellows who whistle and shout: "Come along with me! I know where the Ministers are. Come on!" And all at once columns are formed; they fall into ranks, five or eight abreast, as they learned during their military service or at political demonstrations. The girls take their lovers' arms, the older women stride,

arms swinging, by their husbands' sides. The
brass buttons and the eyes of the armed police glitter angrily at them; but, for the present, they are
allowed to pass. Now Ministers and Ambassadors, Secretaries of State, Generals and Councillors, Lords, Counts, and Grand Dukes, leave their
padded arm-chairs and walk over to the open windows, for the streets are in uproar.

A tramp of marching feet—and we have not yet
given the marching orders! A mustering together
—and no Emperor or President has yet signed
the decree! Do you want to force our hands?

"Peace! Peace! Down with war!"

"Oh, that's it, is it? The damned Socialists!"
The War-Counts of Vienna smile sourly, the
Chancellor in Berlin looks down uneasily, the eyes
of the Grand Dukes dart hatred, the Premier in
London stands silent, and ponders the numbers,
tone, and attitude of the masses, and the Frenchman, himself a son of the people, bites his lips.

"Frieden! Frieden! Wir wollen keinen Krieg!"
comes the shout of a thousand voices from the
Brandenburger Tor, round the corner of the broad
Wilhelmstrasse; and mingling with the scent of
fading limes, an exhalation from the sweat-soaked
garments of the thousand mounts to the windows
of the low, long Ministerial Offices.

"Frieden! Frieden! Nieder mit dem Krieg!" In
the same hour the shout goes up from the Burg-
ring in Vienna; from the steps in front of Parliament's locked and bolted doors it is carried over
the tree-tops of the crowded Volksgarten to the
baroque windows of the Ballhausplatz.

"A bas la Guerre! Vive la paix!" In the same
hour the shout rings over from the two great bridges
on the Seine to the Quai d'Orsay; the tramp of feet
is borne to the dark windows of the Elysée, and the
intoxicating rhythm of the *Marseillaise,* demanding
liberty for the people, rises up to the house of that
same President who is now sailing the high seas,
hoping eagerly for a crisis and reckoning on the
rashness of the Russian generals—it was to the
notes of that very *Marseillaise* that the Imperial
troops paraded before him only the other day.

"Peace! Peace! No war!" In the same hour the
shout goes up from Trafalgar Square; and from
the steps of the greatest of war-memorials the
champions of peace demand peace for the world.

Only in Petersburg, at this hour, has that shouting been silenced; here knout and sabre, iron hoof
and revolver, have dispersed the demonstrators,
trampled them under foot, shot them down. Patriots—yes; *they* may band together and shout to
their hearts' content; at the head of the procession

a car with a general in it, then students and officers, singing and waving flags as they parade through the main streets. It is as well to be prepared for all events; so it has been swiftly and secretly arranged that all letters and telegrams shall be censored.

Behind a veil more holy than that of Saïs, the diplomats of the Great Powers are at work to bring about a war, which, afterwards, these men responsible for it will, without exception, keep at arm's length from their own persons. But they whose death-warrant they were signing in the silence of the Cabinets, they whom the State's unlimited authority compelled to march whenever the drum should roll, they were awake and seemed resolved to defend themselves. Impotent, the Peace Societies of the world raised the voice of idealism; impotent, the Vatican took a few hesitating steps.

While the destiny of Europe was planned almost wholly by one class, another class was called upon to work it out. The mighty had never been able to agree to an arbitral tribunal, but the weak had combined half a century ago in the attempt to save for humanity what they hoped to obtain for their own class. A great vacuum seemed to surround the philosophers and lawgivers, who had proclaimed to the nations their moral ideal of peace;

but history used the sacred egotism of the poor and oppressed to raise a cry against war that should be heard. They had nothing to hope from the rivalry and ambition of the nations, so to their dulled eyes the falsity of banners and sentimental speeches, of glorious victories and heroic songs, was revealed. They groped like men that walk in their sleep, till they clasped the rough, bony fingers of their brothers, the "enemy." Motionless, the uppermost blocks of the artificial pyramids looked fixedly out into the desert; then slowly, inch by inch, groaning under the weight of centuries, the nethermost foundations began to move.

"Because the burden of war falls primarily on the working-classes, and takes from them, not only their bread, but also their blood; because armed peace paralyses the productive forces . . . it is resolved to adhere fully to the Peace Congress in Geneva . . . the purpose of achieving disarmament, and the creation and unification of the free States of Europe, at the earliest possible date."

This, the resolution of the Congress in Lausanne, had been the first protest of the workers against war. Through all strife of factions, all changes of programme, this idea lived on, proclaimed afresh every few years, and gradually winning the millions to its message. Forty years of peace had not lulled these spirits to sleep; now was the moment to let the great No! thrill to the skies.

Count Berchtold's Ultimatum set the alarm ringing among their leaders; and while the diplomats were encoding a thousand telegrams, desperately intent on *not* agreeing, the workers of their countries needed no wires; in the surprise of the first morning, at the same hour, in every centre throughout all the world they dictated to their leaders one thought, the expression of the masses' feelings.

Here are the most important sentences in the manifestoes:

BERLIN.—Appeal by the Committee of the Social Democrat Party: *"Not one drop of a German soldier's blood shall be sacrificed to the lust for power of Austria's tyrants. . . . World war threatens! The ruling classes, who gag, despise, and exploit you in time of peace, now want to turn you into cannon-fodder. Let the ears of the tyrants everywhere hear our shout: 'We will have no war.' International fraternalisation for ever!"*

The *Vorwärts* of July 25th: *"The unscrupulous elements who wield influence and make decisions in the Hofburg at Vienna want war. They want war —the furious shouts of the black-and-yellow chauvinistic Press have been clamouring for it for weeks past. They want war—the Austrian Ultimatum to Serbia makes this clear and unmistakable to the whole world. . . .*

"Because the blood of Franz Ferdinand and his wife has been spilled by the shots of a crazy fanatic, the blood of thousands of workers and peasants is to be spilled; a mad crime is to be capped by a crime still madder. For this Ultimatum, in its tone and its demands, is so shameless that any Serbian Government which should humble itself and bow down before the Note must reckon with the possibility of being kicked out by the people without benefit of clergy.

"It was criminal of the chauvinistic Press in Germany to incite our beloved allies' lust for war to this pitch of fury, and there can be no doubt that Herr von Bethmann-Hollweg has promised Herr Berchtold his backing. But Berlin is playing with fire just as much as Vienna."

The *Leipziger Volkszeitung* of July 24th: *"In Austria the chauvinistic circles are even more completely bankrupt than elsewhere; their nationalist howls are meant to cover their economic ruin, and the loot and murder of war is to fill their pockets."*

VIENNA.—The *Arbeiterzeitung*: *"Every point of this Note of Count Berchtold's reeks of blood, the blood that is to be shed in a cause which could perfectly well be settled in honourable and peaceful fashion. . . . In the name of all those who labour and toil, we throw the responsibility on those who have taken the step which is leading us into the terrible abyss."*

BUDAPEST: *"On the threshold of war we declare in the name of the Hungarian proletariat that our people want no war; and that they hold those who have conjured up this catastrophe to be criminals whom history will pillory."*

PARIS.—Hervé's paper and eleven others, six trade-unions and similar associations issue simultaneously an appeal for a general strike; so do the provinces, in conformity with the resolution just passed by their Congress: *"Of all means to prevent war and bring Governments to arbitration, we hold that of the General Strike in all countries concerned to be the most effectual."*

The *Humanité: "The Austrian Note is terribly severe. It seems deliberately calculated to humiliate the Serbian nation to the dust, or to destroy it. The conditions which Austria wishes to impose on the Serbs are so hard that one must ask whether the clerical and militarist reactionaries in Austria are not wishing for war and desirous of making it unavoidable. That would be the most monstrous of crimes."*

Such are the words, and others like them, that the leaders of the Fourth Estate are calling to each other, this day and the next, from London, Rome, and Bucharest, Berne, and Stockholm, and the cable brings the same resolution across from New Zealand and California. Democratic papers, too, strike a warning note.

PETERSBURG.—The *Retch:* "*The Austro-Hungarian Ultimatum is a retort to the braggart telegrams of the Paris* Matin. *The only possible means for the Triple Entente to avoid being drawn into the conflict is to keep the Serbian question localised and to avoid encouraging Serbia in any way.*"

Even Berlin heaps just accusations on Austria: "*Of all the peoples and Governments whose sundry alliances are drawing them into this frightful situation, not one wants war. The German people is absolutely peaceable, and wishes with all the strength of its soul to see the calamity averted; and we are convinced that in Italy, France, and England the same desire for peace predominates. Neither is the German Government anxious for war, any more than any other of the Governments concerned. There never has been a war so little desired by those who will have to fight it; and yet the world-catastrophe has drawn near, against the wishes of the nations and of their leaders. Whether*

*this was inevitable; whether all had so to come,
shall not be discussed here—German public opinion has, as we have said repeatedly, been confronted with* faits accomplis. *Europe is waiting
for that Prince or Statesman who shall first bring
about an understanding with the belligerent Austria, and then step between the threatened peoples
with practical proposals.*" (Theodor Wolff in the
Berliner Tageblatt.)

On July 30th, an "amateur," not taken seriously
by any of the diplomats, a Berlin doctor named
Arthur Bernstein, had written a prophetic article,
as courageous as it was wise, for the *Berliner Mor-
genpost.* This article, which bore the title "The
Last Warning," was set up, but could not be
printed, because before evening the proclamation
of a *"state of threatening danger of war"* made it
impossible to let the paper appear with such an
article. Five years later, when the type was needed
for other use, this noble document was found and
saved from oblivion. It ran thus:

*"There can no longer be any doubt that the
Nicolaievici on both sides want war. . . . The soldiers scent glory, and since the responsible politicians of Germany are never allowed to have a
word to say when the soldiers are talking, Bethmann and Jagow will acquiesce. A few special*

posts have been pushed forward to weaken Beth-
mann; if he resists for long, there will be volleys
right into the heart of his most intimate private
life. It is dirty, but 'a national necessity' just now.
In a few days more no one will dare to speak the
truth, much less write it.

"Therefore, in the last moment let it be said:
the war-mongers are out in their calculations.
Firstly, there is no such thing as the Triple Al-
liance. Italy will not come in, or, at any rate, not
on our side. If she comes in at all, she will do so on
the side of the Entente. Secondly, England will
not remain neutral, but will support France. . . .
Nor will England suffer German troops to march
through Belgium, which has been generally known
to be our plan of campaign ever since 1907. But,
if England fights against us, the whole English-
speaking world, including more particularly Am-
erica, will come in against us. For England may
not be loved, but she is everywhere respected, which
is, unfortunately, more than can be said of our-
selves. Thirdly, Japan will not attack Russia: she
is more likely to attack us. . . . Fourthly, the Scan-
dinavian States, our 'Germanic' brothers, will sell
us what they can spare, but otherwise will snap
their fingers at us. Fifthly, Austria-Hungary as
a military power is hardly the equal of Serbia and

Roumania. From the economic point of view, she may manage to starve her way through for from three to five years. She can give us nothing. Sixthly, a revolution in Russia will come, if at all, only when the Russians are beaten. . . .

"Our Ambassadors know the situation very exactly. Herr von Bethmann must know it also. It is not to be thought that he is allowing the Empire to be steered by irresponsible persons into three or five years of war, washing his hands, meanwhile, of his responsibility from fear of the threats of the Pan-Germans and militarists. Whether we shall be the victors at the end of the most terrible war that the world will ever have experienced remains to be seen. But even if we win the war, we shall win nothing. . . . Money for war indemnities will be nowhere to be found at the end of the butchery . . . Germany is making the war for nothing, just as she has gone into the war for nothing. A million corpses, two million cripples, and fifty thousand million debts will be the balance-sheet of this 'joyous war'—nothing more."

The *Berliner Lokalanzeiger,* on the other hand —to quote only one example out of a hundred war-mongers—wrote: *"The general impression of the Austro-Hungarian Note may be summed up in the words: sharp, but just. There will perhaps be some who will consider the demands in the Vienna Note too sharp; such a view needs no further answer beyond the facts which have forced the Danube Monarchy to this step. If the belief in the continuance of the monarchic idea in Europe is not to be enfeebled elsewhere, a feeling of justice and of solidarity between States as between monarchs must be sought in those quarters whence Serbia reckons on assistance. Serbia will fulfil Austria's demands, or she will perish."*

The Vienna *Reichspost* even intrigued against Grey's efforts. It printed in huge letters in a special edition—obviously at a hint from Berchtold: *"Austria's sword is drawn, and can no longer be held back, not even by England's attempts at intervention!"*

*   *

As the danger grows, so, in the last days of July, the protests grow more stubborn; but now the differences of national character begin to appear, and the picture is like that of a red fan whose ribs range from orange to mauve. From Russia hardly a voice comes through; the iron grip of the Cossacks is round the throats which would fain cry out. Only in the comparative freedom of the Duma, when war begins, will a voice dare to lift itself up.

The Internationals are silent here, because the

mighty seem resolved on war; in England, too, they are still silent, because she believes herself neutral. The London papers sound no alarm; up to August 4th itself the *Financial News* printed nothing but Stock Exchange and economic news on its first three pages. The little processions through the West End—the Frenchmen of London and a few young men trying side by side to let their flags flutter in the stale city air of hot July —are unimportant. Neither the streets nor the Exchange, neither workers nor employers, here believe seriously in war, and of all counter-arguments a Socialist leaflet selects only that with the broadest appeal:

"Why should we help Russia to rule the Continent? We spent fifty million pounds in the Crimean War because Russia threatened our Indian Empire. These very last weeks, peaceful citizens were being shot down in the streets of her capital. Which is the greater danger for us—sixty-five millions of our own kinsmen, employed in trade and peaceful industry, or one hundred and seventy million Russians, slaves of a corrupt autocracy?"

England's streets will be the last to begin their protests; the last, too, to end them—nay, they will never end them.

In Berlin processions of young people, formed

on the very next day, marched through the Linden
with banners and songs, shouted "Down with Serbia," and were lucky that the police, for the first
time, did not forbid their marching and shouting.
Anyone who saw these youths and adventurers
with their thoughtless high spirits seeking an out-
let soon forgot them if he entered one of the twenty-
seven meetings in which tens of thousands of
workers—sombre, clamorous, and angry—shouted
their applause to this resolution:

*"Austria has declared war against Serbia with
her brutal ... ultimatum. ... With heroic devotion
the Russian proletariat has shown to blood-thirsty
Tsarism the threatening writing on the wall. ... In
flaming words the French worker, like the German,
has protested against the crime of the war-mongers.
It is therefore untrue that the great masses of these
countries are in warlike mood."*

And through thirty-two industrial cities in Germany the same call resounded on the same evening.

But only in closed meetings was the protest allowed—only indoors, that God's ear might not
catch it too easily. Under the open sky nothing
but cheering was permitted, nothing but loud anticipation of the "victor's laurel" for the Kaiser,
nothing but hatred for the brothers across the
political frontier.

For all that, a few hundred men dared to march
from the Friedrichstrasse up the Linden, resolutely singing the workers' song. From the other
side, through the Brandenburger Tor, a procession
of youths marched in to the strains of *Deutschland
über alles*. Mounted police—affray—tumult—the
pavements cleared—the crowd driven off by the
horses' hoofs—fresh demonstrations at the corner
of the Wilhelmstrasse—fresh collisions at the Scha-
dowstrasse. The middle of the roadway of the
Linden shakes under the hoofs of the mounted
police as every fresh reinforcement rides up. Anyone who resists is arrested. The hoofs of the horses,
the batons of the foot-police drive the workers
back, despite their growing excitement—lest any
of the surrounding Embassies should see it from
their balconies and telegraph home that some at
least in Germany are against a war.

So the crowd is driven up along the Linden;
and while the defeated workers retreat northward,
singing still, the others hurry to the Palace. There
the Kaiser has sought protection from his people;
a wide-flung cordon bars access to the Palace.

The voice of love, the songs of his loyal subjects cannot reach their master.

The *Vorwärts* is allowed two days more to shout
the truth abroad: *"There is only one answer to the*

*mobilisation of the Powers; the permanent mobili-
sation of the people."* Finally: *"The German
Kaiser, as Austria's ally, carries in the folds of his
toga peace or war; his is the decision. . . . Unluck-
ily the camarilla of war-mongers, absolutely unscrupulous, is at work here to frustrate all the efforts
of the Government and bring about the monstrosity
—the desolation of Europe!"*

The Kaiser, however, who has not read this, and
has never seen a Socialist face to face in his life,
but has heard about the processions, notes on the
margin of the report: *"This must not be tolerated.
In case it is repeated I shall proclaim a state of
martial law and have the leaders, one and all,
tutti quanti, locked up."*

*   *

What a sign from Heaven itself! Just in these
very days the Socialist leaders from every part of
the earth are assembled in Brussels, where their
headquarters are. In the morning they have debated together, each praising the pressure his colleagues are putting on their respective Governments, and have settled to hold a Congress on
August 9th—and to hold it in Paris, too, so as to
show all the world their unity. But in the evening,
eight thousand workmen of Brussels crowd to-

gether in the huge but stiflingly hot arena, and point out to one another the leaders on the platform. That one there, the President, is Vandervelde, their own countryman; they all know him. He is rather pale and thoughtful to-night, like Troelstra beside him. But there is Keir Hardie's resolute, idealistic face; he bears assurance of England's desire for peace; and beside him is Rubinovitch, who has just been helping to carry through the great strike in Petersburg. There is Haase, the leader of the Germans: very intelligent, showing, perhaps, more suffering than passion in his face; on him, as head of the strongest Socialistic party in the world, all eyes are fixed; he tells with pride the story of yesterday's events in Berlin; his brethren's clamour for peace offers a guarantee against all Tirpitzes and Berchtolds.

But lo! Who mounts the platform after him? A thickset man with a leonine head—one might take him for a Viking, so blonde and stalwart is his form. But only hear his voice, when the clamour of the thousands is stilled! For, because they love him, they keep him waiting for whole minutes before they will let him speak. This is their leader, this man is Europe's conscience to-day. He comes from the land of revolution and liberty, for them he fights in the tangle of bewildered parties at

JEAN LÉON JAURÈS

Leader of the Socialists in France

home; he calls them out under the sky of every
land. He is uncrowned king of the millions of both
hemispheres, knight of fraternity and minstrel of
brotherly love. He is the tribune. Jaurès!

There he stands, not tall but powerfully built; a
man in the middle fifties. Is this a modern
prophet? Is he a friend of humanity? He does
not look like a fanatic, he wears no aura of tragedy; what fills him seems to be joy of life and the
desire to bring it to many brothers. A penniless
youth, helped through his student years by kind
patrons, Deputy and Professor of Philosophy at
twenty-five, he has garnered an enormous harvest
of knowledge that he may prove to himself and
his friends what his heart knew from the beginning. But his joy in humanity—the deepest feeling in this childlike lion—would stream out most
powerfully when he spoke to others, to one or two,
or a thousand. Even as he loves France, where he
grew up in the beautiful Languedoc country, as
warmly and as instinctively does he love Europe;
he cannot understand why its various parts should
fight against each other. He turned Socialist to
bring peace, not war; for justice's sake, not hate's;
and that rings out in his speeches.

What will he say in this hour of destiny?

"Our part is an easier one than that of our Ger-

*man comrades. We do not need to force peace
upon our country. She wants it herself. I, who
have never feared to draw down on my head the
hate of Chauvinists because I wished to bring Germany and France nearer to each other, have the
right to-day to testify aloud for my country. I
declare it solemnly: the Government of France in
this moment wishes for peace. England's admirable Government is paving the way for reconciliation, and urging wisdom and patience in Russia.
Were she, however, to fail, and were Russia to
march to-morrow, the French workman would say:
We know no secret treaty, only the public treaty
with humanity and civilisation.*

"*Time and again the noble German Socialists
have been held up to us in France as models. Yesterday the lying veil was rent; our comrades of
Berlin demonstrated in their thousands. Never
has German labour done humanity a greater service.*

"*French Socialists were among them, and
shouted* 'Nieder mit dem Kriege' *in the procession
on the Linden. . . . If mechanical force and the in-
toxication of the first battles prevail; if the absolute masters succeed in inflaming the masses until
death and misery show their hideous faces everywhere, and typhus rounds off the work of the guns,*

*then all the armies will turn against their rulers
and ask: 'Where are your reasons for these heaped
corpses?' Then Revolution unleashed will say to
them: 'Begone, and pray to God and man for
mercy!' But if we succeed in abating the storm,
then the peoples will cry: 'Let us forbid this
spectre to rise every six months from the grave
to affright the world!'*

*"I thank our German comrades in the name of
the French, and I swear: We will continue to support them like brothers against the war-mongers'
Attila campaign, true till death."*

The arena shakes with mighty cheering. Eight
thousand men have left their seats; they are ready
to stretch their limbs—for their souls are refreshed.
This is the truth! So they all feel. Did none mark
the last word—the word at the end of the speech—
"Death!"?

Never again will Jean Jaurès uplift his lion's
voice to the multitude.

*   *

Paris has a new sensation. Not since men fought
duels for and against Dreyfus; not for twenty
years had Paris been so passionately absorbed by
any one event as by the trial of Madame Caillaux,
wife of the former Minister-President, who had

shot the editor of the *Figaro* out of revenge for his
political campaign—not, indeed, that that was her
only reason. While Europe was groaning under
the Ultimatum, like a nightmare fallen on its summer slumber, the Parisians were all agog to hear
the speeches for the prosecution and the defence,
and the papers daily gave pride of place to the
poses of the elegant murderess, in long series of
pictures, taking precedence of the telegrams from
Vienna and Belgrade. Not all knew that in the
last analysis the political consequences of the murder of Calmette and those of the murder of the
Archduke coincided, and that the acquittal of
Madame Caillaux meant at the same time the
death sentence of France's love of peace, standing
there in the dock at her side.

Fatigue, and a desire to be free to consider the
new and larger event, helped to influence public
opinion, to which the judges were obliged to listen,
since the brothers of the Berlin shouters had also
paraded the boulevards of Paris.

The Socialists called up their men:

*"Since Saturday a hypnotised crowd has been
surging through the Grands Boulevards, crying 'A
Berlin! Vive la guerre!' If these madmen are not
forced into silence to-day, all is up to-morrow.
Out, then, this evening at half-past eight, all as-*

semble in front of the offices of the Matin *and cry
'Down with War!'"*

Next day: appeal to proclaim a general strike in
Paris. This is an historic day; this morning, for
the first time, the voice of a conscience-torn Socialist has been raised—a Socialist torn between
fatherland and humanity. Seven years ago in
Stuttgart he triumphed: *"The French General
Staff has been morally disarmed by us anti-mili-
tarists; it knows that war would mean the rising of
the proletariat."* Hervé it is, and now his outpour-
ings in two great articles in his paper mark the
beginning of a crisis in the International, the end
of which will, in a few days, decide Europe's fate.
Hear his voice to-day: What moves him? The
vacillating emotions of a tormented soul? Or a belief that Germany will attack France?

*"What? Our fair dream of an international
general strike against war—where is it now? We
had dreamed of leading the peoples against their
Governments, to force them into arbitration of
their conflicts. But our wings are broken by the
impact of hard reality, and we have fallen back to
earth, to our native earth, with but one thought—
to defend it in this moment, as our fathers did,
against the brutality of invasion! . . . Were it but a
war to defend a little, oppressed nation! But the*

stake is the prestige of the Tsar, the honour of the Russian Government! Rabelais, Voltaire, Victor Hugo, would burst out laughing in their graves at those words—the honour of Nicholas cannot endure that Serbia should be touched. The honour of our noble ally was not so nicely attuned when he throttled Finland, enslaved the Poles and Jews! . . . Our group in the Chamber believes that Russia's intervention could only increase the danger without saving poor Serbia. This would be merely playing the game of the German imperialists, and making them feel that their hour had come!"

"The fatherland is in danger!" he cries the next day. *"The fatherland of the Revolution is in danger! Here in Paris we have already cut the verse about the Generals out of the song of the International, and the purified International is now nothing other than the* Marseillaise, *which our fathers sang a hundred years ago!"* Can we hear through the brilliant phrases the convulsions of unrest? *"The fatherland of the Revolution is in danger!"*

Yet the masses still seem to be firm. A giant meeting of the Confédération Générale is announced in Paris for the evening after the Berlin processions. It is forbidden at the last moment, *"because the speakers wish to discuss methods of preventing mobilisation."* Is that an echo of Wilhelm's voice? Have the gentlemen of the Republic read his Imperial notes? All attempts to prevent war are forbidden by order of the Government. Form no groups, you pacifists! Disperse, you brothers! Our prestige is in danger!

The next day an illustrated paper in Paris has a page showing the Kaiser on the left-hand side, Poincaré on the right, both returning to their residences accompanied by the applause of the multitudes. Even to-day the nation of each hopes that each will bring it peace.

CHAPTER X

THE CONCERT OF EUROPE

BACK to the stifling air of the Cabinets! Let us hear what is making the leaders of the States so bitter! Will the spectacle of high destiny disarm our hearts, move us to pity for the wretched creatures who seek to escape its course? Will the inquiry reveal weighty problems which only force can solve?

Much remains hidden; but what emerges is nothing more than the mutual fear of the opposing groups, magnified to immensity. What the score or so of gentlemen now weighing the destiny of Europe have to say to one another will never be tragic— lamentable at most; never lofty, only ridiculous. If the countless men and women who, five years later, after losing their sons and husbands, sought in the archives of their nations to find comfort in the vision of an innocent fatherland fighting for existence against the devilish machinations of its enemies, could read this international truth, they all would simply break out into curses that the lives of those dearest to them, and millions more, should have been destroyed to no purpose for the criminal frivolity of a few Counts in Vienna, for the heedlessness of German statesmen, for the ambition of Russian Grand Dukes, for the nervous weakness of crowned cousins—for men who in guilt and greed, in aims and desires, in gifts and vices nowhere surpassed the average, and were great in only one thing: in the means by which they betrayed and destroyed the unsuspecting millions.

*   *

Count Berchtold smiled. He had learnt to hide disappointment and joy alike behind the impassive mask of the grand seigneur; even when his thoroughbreds made a bad start, he smiled pleasantly in the grand-stand. Similarly, he showed to no one how awkward for his plans was the triumphant return of the race-horse which he had sent to Serbia. Sly old Pashitch had admitted defeat, the King of a free country had pledged himself to pronounce public condemnation of the ideals of his race and nation, to dismiss defenders of their fatherland at the orders of a truculent neighbour.

European statesmen had breathed more freely
when they read Pashitch's submission, the morning
after the last scene in Belgrade.

Berlin alone was ill served. Twice already it
had been unscrupulously deceived by its ally, for
Berchtold was a pupil of Metternich, while Bethmann was no pupil of Bismarck. With intent to
deceive, Berchtold had hidden from Berlin the
official statement that the results of the Serbian
inquiry had been *"scanty,"* so that Berlin believed
in the *"sufficiency"* of the material, the only thing
which could even partly justify the Ultimatum in
the eyes of Europe. Similarly Berchtold had assured Berlin that *"Austria-Hungary has no intention of making any territorial acquisition,"* but had
hidden the fact that the Cabinet in Vienna, again
contrary to Tisza's warnings, had determined on
*"reducing the area of Serbia in favour of other
States."*

Now neither Austria through her Ambassador
in Berlin, nor the German Ambassador in Vienna,
sent the text of the Serbian answer to the German
Government; and only when twenty-four precious
hours had gone by did the Serbian Chargé d'Affaires bring it himself, so that only then could it be
despatched to the Kaiser at Potsdam. It was ten
o'clock in the evening when this very crucial his-

torical document arrived. The Monarch postponed reading it.

The next morning he reads the document; relief
succeeds to astonishment, he breathes more freely.
God has saved him once more from the necessity
of making war. The Divine Hand has visibly
guided the Serbian pen. Has not the Kaiser
proved that his soul is firm? Has he not as good
as thrown down the gauntlet? Vienna has conquered, Bucharest has received its warning, Sofia
has been encouraged. One more honourable gesture, and the Nibelungen troth has saved the aged
ally.

The Kaiser writes in the margin: *"A brilliant
performance for a time-limit of only forty-eight
hours. This is more than one could have expected!
A great moral victory for Vienna; but with it every
reason for war drops away, and Giesl might have
remained quietly in Belgrade! On the strength of
this I should never have ordered mobilisation!"* At
the same time he writes to Jagow; the final points
could be settled by negotiation, but Austria must
receive honourable satisfaction, she must first set
her foot on foreign soil and hold Belgrade in her
hand as a pledge. On this basis he is prepared to
offer his mediation.

A nervous man, afraid of seeming afraid, with

the vocabulary of a typical officer; a despotic ruler
accustomed to call a halt whenever he desires—
thus the sick soul of this man, who is always
swayed by appearances, is driven by one impulse
to threats, by a fresh impulse to yielding. At the
head of a factory, a company, or a family he would
have proved lacking in stability; and he could have
ensured it for his great Empire only by choosing
manfully independent ministers to serve him.

In these days he is purely peaceable; what
further remarks fall from his hand in the patient
white margins of the documents? Beside an article which warned him to beware of Russia's attitude: *"I could not assume that the Tsar would
place himself on the side of bandits and regicides.
. . . Germans are incapable of such a point of
view; it is Slavonic or Latin."*

Meanwhile, Count Berchtold has circulated a
so-called "dossier" against Serbia—it might equally
be called a *note explicative,* or given another name
out of the dictionary of Rococo. Living wholly in
the euphemistic spirit of that age, this shadow of
a seigneur loves such phrases, which reveal the
vision of the world-war as it appeared to him
through the windows of his Cabinet. *"This is the
first time since the foundation of the Triple Alliance that the lists have been joined on a large*

*scale." "Take notice, pray, that this remark is
made without hostile intention against Russia."*
And as, after all, everything is at stake, he speaks
of a last attempt to *"stay"* the European war.

This style smacks of its origin; its graceful
curves and swoops are quite in the mode of the
eighteenth-century palace in which it is penned;
and reading it, one can understand what embarrassment arose there over the question who should
"hand in" the declaration of war. Giesl had had
to leave at once; to send it by post would be un-
safe, since receipt might be denied; a *parlemen-
taire* would not be *de rigueur* before the declaration
of war. Finally, the simple and suitable way was
chosen. It was wired in French to Belgrade via
Bucharest on July 28th at 11 A.M. *"The Royal
Serbian Government not having answered in a
satisfactory manner the note of July 10–23, 1914,
presented by the Austro-Hungarian Minister at
Belgrade, the Imperial and Royal Government
are thus pledged to see to the safeguarding of
their rights and interests, and, with this object, to
have recourse to force of arms. Austria-Hungary
consequently considers herself henceforward in a
state of war with Serbia.*

*"Count Berchtold, Austro-Hungarian Minister
of Foreign Affairs."*

The responsibility for this first declaration of war rests on Vienna alone. For in the same hour when the news reached the Foreign Office in Berlin of this step, which had, indeed, been expected but might still have been stopped, a telegram was being drafted to Tschirschky, to *"mediate for peace"* according to the Kaiser's orders. A few hours later Berchtold informed Berlin that the last English proposal for mediation had likewise been outstripped by events, i. e. by his own action. Bethmann, on the other hand, telegraphed to the four great Cabinets that Germany was *"continually endeavouring to bring Vienna to an open exchange of views with Petersburg."*

From now onward, as peace lies prostrate, her conqueror, Count Berchtold, is *"in very good spirits and proud of the countless telegrams of congratulation that are coming to him from every quarter."* The Count's pleasant feelings, however, were of all too brief duration: two years later, when someone asked him how the war was going, he answered thus: *"Leave me in peace. I got sick of the war long ago!"*

The whole Austrian Press, which had hardly been able to wait for the last few weeks, rushes into print with a flourish of bellicose enthusiasm. *"Serbia must be trampled under foot."*

This, the first day of Europe's war, is also the
first on which God is mobilised, for the old Emperor is *"conscious of the momentous character of
my decisions, and have taken them trusting in
God's justice."* He is followed two days later by
the German God in the Kaiser's telegram: *"I join
my prayers with yours that God may stand by us."*
The Russian reaches the mark only third; the Tsar
says to the German Ambassador, pointing to Heav-
en: *"Only One can help us."* After these three
invocations they pay as little attention to God as
to men.

So it is in God's name that the first shots go up
to Heaven this night. Only a few shots, but their
echo will not die away! Europe has become a land
of mountains; barriers on barriers in their thousands have towered up in this first night of war
between the peoples; no one can look over into his
neighbour's valley, so high stand the rocks and
glaciers between the men who even yesterday, despite their many tongues, understood one another so
easily, exchanged merchandise and labour, thoughts
and women. Europe has become a land of Alps,
and for that reason, the countless echoes of this first
shot will take four years before they die away at
last.

A Satyric Drama follows the first Serbian shots;

on the 27th, when everything depended for Count
Berchtold on persuading his hesitating Emper-
or to sign the declaration of war, he said in his
"Urgent Report" (which was committed to paper) :
*"According to a report from the Commander of
the Fourth Corps, Serbian troops have fired on
our troops from Danube steamers at Temes-Kubin.
The fire was returned and a considerable skirmish
developed.* De facto *hostilities have thus been
opened.* Berchtold therefore added the following
words at the end of the declaration of war: *"The
more so as Serbian troops have already attacked a
detachment of Imperial and Royal troops at Temes-Kubin."* This was so plausible that the old
gentleman could not but believe it, and signed.

Hardly had the Count received the precious signature when he scratched the shots of the alleged
Serbian aggressors out of the declaration of war,
their original plausibility being hard to maintain.
He excused himself to the Emperor on the 29th
with the words: *"Since the information regarding
the skirmish at Temes-Kubin has not been confirmed . . . I have taken it on myself . . . to
erase the sentence about the attack from the declaration of war against Serbia."* So Count Berchtold
had not merely deceived his allies, but also his own

Imperial master, by concealing from him at least the fact that this reason for war had vanished.

*   *

In Berlin the negotiations were conducted by the Ambassadors of France and Great Britain. Jules Cambon, short of stature, small-eyed, lynx-like, is the man who knows everything that is going on in Berlin, much of what is going on in Paris, and most of what is going on in London, where his brother, who is Ambassador there, keeps him informed. A man of the world, no chauvinist, a democrat, not intimidated by the Byzantine atmosphere of Berlin, a true Parisian, this popular Frenchman enjoys his life here far too well to make unnecessary trouble, and hopes not to have to leave the fine Palace on the Pariser Platz for many years to come. His English colleague, Sir Edward Goschen, more reserved, more cultivated, respected rather than liked, shares this ambition, and the two between them have smoothed over many a quarrel.

The same thing may be said of their two colleagues in Vienna, where old M. Dumaine breathes the semi-French air of the Hapsburg Court with no less pleasure than does the British Ambassador,

Sir Maurice de Bunsen, a man of German descent, grandson of a former Prussian Minister in London. All four, particularly the two Englishmen, are occupied during these days in attempting to secure acceptance for England's various proposals for a Conference, which come in rapid succession. When the Viennese rejected the *"spectre of a Conference,"* alleging the disagreeable associations of that word, Grey proposed conversations between the four Ambassadors. "If I get them all at one table," he thought, "no one will stand up to shoot so much as a revolver."

Accordingly, Goschen had begun by putting the suggestion forward and had received no definite refusal. The next day, however, feelings changed between morning and afternoon, and Jagow said to Goschen: *"That would practically amount to a Court of Arbitration!"* In the evening Cambon comes again. He warns the German Secretary of State, with whom he has been on good terms for years: but in vain.

"Are you bound to follow Austria everywhere with your eyes blindfolded? Have you not taken note of the reply of Serbia this morning?"

"I have not yet had time."

"I regret it. You would see that except on some points of detail Serbia has yielded entirely. It

*appears, then, that you might advise Austria to
be content.   Or does Germany wish for war?"*

*"I know what is in your mind, but it is wholly
incorrect."*

Cambon speaks of responsibility, and prepares
to leave; then he turns once again to the German
and speaks boldly, but in a more friendly tone than
Berthelot had adopted yesterday in Paris.

*"This morning I had the impression that the
hour of détente had struck.   Take action in Vienna
to hasten the progress of events!   It is a matter of
importance not to allow time for the development
in Russia of one of those currents of opinion which
carry all before them."*

Three minutes later the Frenchman is sitting
with the Englishman in the Embassy, three houses
away.   The latter listens to him, and yet he may
not speak:

*"My dear friend, I think just as you do about
England; unhappily, however, I have no authority
to say so."*

*   *

The tragic climax: Grey confronted with Hamlet's riddle, which ceaselessly torments him. Again
and again during these days he has warned the
German Ambassador not to let Austria fire the

first shot. Now, on the same day (July 27th), almost in the same hour as that conversation in Berlin, the Russian in London urges him to show his hand at last:

"In German and Austrian circles the impression prevails that England will stand aside in any event. This must have a deplorable effect in Berlin."

Grey: *"Churchill has given orders to the First Fleet not to disperse for manœuvre leave. Surely that will be plain enough for Germany. Nevertheless, you must not take my reference to this to mean that anything more than diplomatic action is promised."*

One hour later the Russian Ambassador's cousin, Count Mensdorff, from Vienna, is sitting on the same chair beside Grey's table. To him Grey says:

"Our First Fleet, which is concentrated, as it happens, at Portland, will not disperse. There is no menace in what we are doing here. Owing to the possibility of a European conflagration, it is impossible for us to disperse our forces at this moment. We should not think of calling up reserves at this moment. I give this as an illustration of the anxiety that we are feeling."

A painful situation for a Minister who wishes honestly for peace; and yet, with his reservations and hints, has become suspect to both sides and at last to himself.

*   *

Petersburg: the English Ambassador here is in the same dilemma.   Since that first luncheon *à trois* the Franco-Russian duet has not ceased to din its refrain into her ears.   Next day they sit, again *à trois,* this time in Sazonov's room.

Sazonov: *"You will not win Germany for the cause of peace unless you proclaim your solidarity with us and France openly.   This is a crisis in which the liberty of Europe itself is at stake."*

Buchanan, still reluctantly repeating his instructions against his own wishes: *"You are mistaken if you believe that England would be advancing the cause of peace by informing the German Government that in lending Austria support she would have us, as well as France and Russia, against her."*

Paléologue gets up, points with a true French gesture at the picture of Gortchakoff hanging on the wall, and cries: *"In July* 1870, *on this very spot, my dear Sir George, Prince Gortchakoff said to your father, who was warning him of the danger of German ambition: 'There's nothing to worry Russia in the increase of German power!'*

*Don't let England make the same mistake to-day
which cost Russia so dear then!"*

Buchanan answers quietly, with a weary smile:
"You know you're preaching to the converted."

The two allies fall silent, and rack their brains
how the conversations in London can be
strengthened at this point.

A second group in Petersburg: The German
and Austrian Ambassadors, mutually mistrustful,
receive very different treatment from Sazonov,
adapted to their respective characters; the official
manners of the German, Count Pourtalès, get on
Sazonov's nerves and lead him to adopt a sharper
tone than is desirable between mediators. Count
Szápáry's Hungarian courtesy seduces him into
pleasanter speech than is usual among enemies.
Incidentally, the Russian enjoys insulting each
country in the presence of the Ambassador of the
other.

Sazonov did not yet wish for war, to which he
could resort whenever he would, but the intran-
sigence of the Central Powers had provoked him
into sharp words against the Germans.

"You are blinded by your hatred of Austria,"
said Pourtalès.

*"Hatred is no part of my character, Count Pour-
talès. I feel no hatred towards Austria, only con-*

tempt. We know Austria's far-reaching plans. First Serbia is to be eaten up, then will come Bulgaria's turn, until we have them on the Black Sea."

"You know, Your Excellency, that this is only a punitive expedition, and that Austria has no idea of making any territorial acquisitions."

Two days later:

"You must intervene in Vienna. Help us to build a golden bridge," says Sazonov.

"And meanwhile you are going on arming?" asks Pourtalès.

"Certain preparations, to avoid being surprised; no mobilisation. We have determined to wait until Austria adopts a hostile attitude towards us."

"Here I must warn you, with all possible emphasis; such measures are extremely dangerous and may easily provoke counter-measures."

With these words Count Pourtalès had hit off the war spirit better than he knew. They were a prophetic characterisation of the automatism, the sullen tenacity, the revengefulness of that mighty and complex machine which ended by escaping from its makers' control. At the same time the words described the Russian machine which, vaster and cruder than the German, was destined, a few days later, to begin revolving at the same moment as the other, because the masters of each had pressed a button. Count Pourtalès, Junker and officer, has condemned the system which he serves.

On the following day (July 27th) Sazonov is more conciliatory. *"Could not Austria moderate the form of her demands to a certain extent?"*

"I can offer you no prospect of this at all; I can only advise you, in case you believe you have reason to hope, as a result of your conversations with Count Szápáry, to address yourself to Vienna direct."

The reader breathes more freely: "Direct, at last!" For while Europe trembles for the fate of millions, its Cabinets do not speak "direct." They never speak of answer, of negotiation, of danger of war, but always of Notes, of conversations, complications, enunciations of force—and no one in these stuffy rooms considers how the reports of such negotiations lead the peoples astray, how they cloud the brains even of those engaged in them.

Sazonov is ready to take up the German idea at once; it was, indeed, his own. Coming from him, however, it would have weakened his position against Vienna, while as emanating from Germany it is already half Viennese. At the same time, the Russian has improved his position in relation to England; he has shown that things can be arranged even without Grey. He wires at once to Vienna.

Now Sazonov chats pleasantly enough with the Hungarian, tells a few lies about his sympathies for Austria, takes up the Ultimatum, and after the Hungarian has made an official declaration that he is *"not authorized to discuss and interpret this document,"* so that the conversation must be taken as never having taken place, the two discuss Vienna's demands to Serbia like sensible men. The Russian thinks seven of them acceptable, for the other three he suggests changes and adds:

"After all, it is only a question of words!"

Sazonov, who at this hour has not yet been informed of Serbia's surrender, wishes no more than to rob Vienna of her full *"diplomatic success"* (revenge for Buchlau!), and at the end expresses himself "delighted" by his conversation with the enemy.

"Only three points," think both, and both telegraph to Vienna. Sazonov has the edict of mobilisation in his pocket; this makes him feel that his position is a strong one. Now he reads Serbia's answer. It is, to be sure, somewhat annoying that the matter looks like getting settled without him; but he sees that there are really only two points left at issue, and so hopes the more confidently for speedy agreement from Vienna. All declare them-

selves delighted with the new *direct* method of
negotiation now in prospect; Grey calls it *"better
than his own."*

They do not know that Berchtold, whose own
Ambassador has just reached agreement in Petersburg, is engaged at the self-same hour in drafting
the declaration of war to Serbia, because he means
to have war in any circumstances.

*   *

Is Vienna to have waited in vain, for the sixth
time, for a pretext to act against Serbia? Never!
Therefore these days witness the summary and un-
varied rejection of all proposals, whatever their
origin. Already we can count four such: Russia's proposal to increase the time-limit of the
Ultimatum, Grey's first proposal for a Conference.
Now Russia's proposal for *"conversations"* is also
categorically rejected, and when finally the Serbs
send word that they might accept the last two
points also, Berchtold replies that, even so, several
questions would remain to be settled. In any case,
Austria must lay down quite other conditions after
the declaration of war than before it.

"If Vienna is a system of fortifications,"
think the foreigners, "we must begin by bombarding Fort Berlin. Will Berlin prove equally im-

pervious to assault?" Berlin's attitude towards
the proposals for mediation is as follows:

First proposal: When the Russian Chargé d'Affaires asks for a prolongation of the time-limit,
he is put off, in order that Jagow may be able to
say, at the hour of its expiration:

"I fear it is too late."

*"Then is Austria determined on war against
Serbia?"*

*"This is not a war; it is a punitive expedition to
settle a local question."*

When the English Ambassador, at Grey's
orders, proposes the same extension of the time-
limit for Serbia, Jagow replies that he sent on
the proposal to his Ambassador in Vienna *"immediately"* (at 10 A.M.) with orders to discuss it
with Berchtold. In reality Jagow wired to Tschirschky at four in the afternoon, precisely because
he knew that the time-limit expired at six and that
Berchtold was in Ischl, so that it was then too late
to alter anything.

Second proposal: Grey sends invitations to a
conference, Berlin declares it cannot *"interfere
with"* its ally.

Third proposal: Russia asks that Vienna be
urged to consent to direct conversations. Jagow
gives a cold consent but half revokes it with the

words: *"We can, however, in no case put pressure on Austria."*

Fourth proposal: This time Grey suggests making the Serbian answer the basis of negotiations. Bethmann turns the paper over in his hand, "Very awkward! What is to be done now?" He gives the Austrian Ambassador such instructions that the latter can telegraph to Vienna with an easy mind: *"The German Government gives the most binding assurance that it in no way identifies itself with the proposals; that, on the contrary, it is decidedly opposed to accepting them, and is passing them on only in order to satisfy England's request."* He adds, indeed, that *"at each request from England Germany will inform her most expressly that she cannot in any way support such demands for interference with Austria-Hungary."* Bethmann's own feelings and thoughts on that day (July 27th) are shown by the commentary which he telegraphs to Vienna at midnight.

At this hour the eyes of the gentlemen in the Wilhelmstrasse begin to open. Enlightenment comes through a fresh alarmist telegram from Lichnowsky: *"If it comes to war in these circumstances we shall have England against us."* Now, at last, Bethmann begins to see the danger of his blind support of Berchtold. Instead, however, of putting the brake on hard, he wires to his Ambassador in Vienna no more than this: *"After refusing one English proposal for a Conference, it would be impossible to waive* à limine *this English suggestion also. By refusing every proposition for mediation, we should be held responsible for the conflagration by the whole world, and be set forth as the original instigators of the war. That would also make our position impossible for our own country, where we must appear as having been forced into the war. . . . Therefore, we cannot refuse the mediator's rôle . . . especially as London and Paris continue to make their influence felt in Petersburg."*

"We must appear"—a fragrant blossom of diplomacy so long as it flowers in the protecting shade of cipher! A stinking weed when once history has felled the wood and let daylight in on it! When Bethmann sent on the English proposal in a tone which unmistakably advised rejection of it, he thought to create an historic document for Germany. When the papers came to light five years later, it had turned into an historic document against Bethmann.

To make sure that Vienna does not swoon from the shock of this, he adds that Berlin is *"decidedly opposed to mediation by London, and only passes*

*on the suggestion in order to satisfy England's
request."* And when the next day even the peace-
loving Kaiser Wilhelm himself urges him to force
Berchtold to satisfy himself with *"a pledge,"* Bethmann closes his instructions to Vienna with the historic words:

*"The case is solely one of finding a way to
realise Austria's desired aim that could cut the
vital cord of the Greater Serbia propaganda without at the same time bringing on a world war, and
if the latter cannot be avoided in the end, of im-
proving the conditions we shall have to wage it in,
so far as is possible."*

Though this be madness, there is method in it.
Nowhere do we get such a revelation of mediocre
superficiality as in this bureaucratic sentence of
the Chancellor's. Unlike the Generals, he is by no
means desirous of war; but he sees it coming, and
yet, even after his Kaiser's decisive change of
front, lifts no hand to stop it, and thinks only of
shifting the blame ingeniously on to others *"if a
world war cannot be avoided in the end."*

*   *

Tsarskoe Selo is in warlike mood. Austria's
silence and Berlin's evasive answers have swept
the obstacles from the Generals' path; Sazonov,

who is beginning to feel that he is getting left behind, need delay no longer, and days after the
Generals have begun their own preparations, himself votes for mobilisation, beginning with the
South-Eastern Governments: Moscow, Kiev,
Odessa, and Kazan. The Generals have gone forth.
Yesterday they stripped a German steamer of its
wireless; to-day, on complaints being lodged, they
have given it back.

Such is the feeling when a telegram arrives
from the German Kaiser. It had been requested
through private channels three days earlier, but not
sent off; not until yesterday, when the Kaiser decided to come round and Bethmann wanted a
guilty Russia, did he submit a draft to his master
conceived on this basis. In this telegram the Kaiser calls on the Tsar to help him smooth the quarrel
over, as both have reason to punish regicides.

On the 29th General von Chelius meets Prince
Trubetzkoi, a dignitary of the Russian Court, and
the latter says:

*"God be praised, a telegram from your Kaiser,
but I fear it is too late."*

Chelius: *"You must not be surprised if the
German forces are mobilised, since you have already mobilised yourself."*

Trubetzkoi stands horror-struck and says that

he must go to Peterhof. Whereupon the subtle Chelius records his impression that *"they have mobilised here from the dread of events, without any aggressive intentions, and now are frightened at what they have brought about."*

This conclusion—which, psychologically, is absolutely correct—explains Russia's attitude during these days without really condemning it, and is the more important because it comes from a German general and is confirmed by the German Kaiser with *"Right, that is it."* At the same time, it is a perfect explanation of the psychological state of Europe's Cabinets. Here, even before the outbreak of war, Chelius found the formula for the fear felt by all of all, for the frivolity of a few who let loose an avoidable war, and consequently for the necessity of a tribunal which Europe could invoke when next her statesmen lose their nerve.

Even on the 30th Europe could have been saved. All the Powers had recognised Austria's right to give Serbia a lesson, and to occupy portions of her territory temporarily as a guarantee for the execution of such of her demands as did not infringe Serbia's sovereignty. Berchtold promised this to the Cabinets; but his real purpose was to destroy Serbia. In this way he presented his enemies with their chance of attacking Austria. At

COUNT VON BETHMANN HOLLWEG

Secretary of State in the Cabinet of the Kaiser, 1914–

the same time he smiled on everyone, and betrayed his allies no less than his enemies, so that at last even Bethmann broke out into violent language to Tschirschky on the 29th:

"I regard the attitude of the Austrian Government . . . with increasing astonishment. At Petersburg it announces its territorial disinterestedness; us it leaves entirely at sea regarding its programme. Rome is put off with meaningless phrases on the compensation question. At London Mensdorff is giving away portions of Serbia to Bulgaria and Albania, and placing himself in direct opposition to Vienna's solemn declarations at Petersburg. I must draw from these contradictions the conclusion that . . . the Government at Vienna is entertaining plans which it finds advisable to keep secret from us in order to ensure itself of German support in any event. . . ."

This Viennese system of treachery gave the eager Russians welcome excuse to ensnare their weak sovereign.

The Tsar, the most peaceable man in the world amid all the clamour round him, would be as glad as the Kaiser to retreat; past midnight on the 29th he telegraphs to his cousin uneasily: *"I foresee that very soon I shall be overwhelmed by the pressure brought upon me."*

Are these words touching or ridiculous? The most powerful monarch in the world, the last despot of history, makes confessions of his impotence; and its recipient, when he laughs over this weakness, does he see how akin his own situation is to that of his cousin? On the evening of the same day the Tsar points out the most sensible course: *"It would be right to give the Austro-Serbian problem to The Hague Conference. . . . Your loving Nicky."*

Soon the King of England, in his turn, will enter the electric circuit of the telegrams, and we shall see the three crowned cousins, who call each other Georgie, Willy, and Nicky, on the threshold of the world catastrophe; heirs of families once mighty, one of whom ran away at the end, while a second was shot in a cellar.

As the Hungarian is leaving Sazonov's room on the 28th, he meets the Frenchman in the antechamber. The latter asks: *"Have you any better news from Vienna?"*

"No, I know nothing more. . . . The machine is in motion."

Another unwitting accuser of Europe.

The Hungarian departs. The German arrives. The Frenchman makes him a bombastic speech in the antechambers; the German answers:

*"I call God to witness! Germany is peace-loving!
History will prove that right is on our side, and
our conscience has nothing to reproach us with."*

*"Have we already got so far as to have to in-
voke the judgment of history?"*

*"We cannot and will not leave our allies in the
lurch!"*

The Frenchman lets the German precede him to
the Minister. Outside, the Englishman says to
the Frenchman:

*"The situation is worse. I don't doubt that Rus-
sia will go through with it; she is thoroughly in
earnest. I have just been begging Sazonov not to
consent to any military measure which Germany
could call provocative. The German Government
must be saddled with all the responsibility and all
the initiative. English opinion will accept the idea
of intervening in the war only if Germany is in-
dubitably the aggressor. . . . Please talk to Sazonov to that effect."*

What this Englishman is thinking to-day in
Petersburg—are they not precisely the same
thoughts, and expressed in the same words, as the
German Chancellor will be telegraphing to Vienna
this evening? The rôle of the victim of aggression;
the ideal of all war-loving diplomats in Europe!
The doctors have been making each other nervous

for eight years and eight days past; now they all give peace her death-warrant, and set to polishing up their diagnoses, in order to prove themselves right at the autopsy.

Now Sazonov receives his last visitor, his friend the Frenchman, who finds him agitated, learns details, and warns him:

"The least imprudence on your part will lose us England's help."

Sazonov: *"That's my opinion too; but our General Staff are getting restless, and even now I am having great difficulty in holding them in."*

In the course of the next day Vienna finally rejects the "conversations." Now Sazonov wants to play for safety. He receives the Ambassadors in succession.

At first he speaks sensibly with the Hungarian, who has been vainly advising Vienna to give way and now has the most unpleasant of all the parts to play in Petersburg.

Sazonov: *"We shall carry through partial mobilisation to-day, but these troops are not intended to attack you. They will only be kept in readiness. A measure of precaution, since Austria is in advance of us and can, in any case, mobilise more quickly."*

The Hungarian: *"Nevertheless, it will make the*

deepest impression in Austria." Sazonov gives him further reassurances. During this *"confidential exchange of views"* the telephone rings: shots have been fired against Belgrade. All at once Sazonov is a changed man; now he bursts out violently against the Ambassador:

"The Tsar is quite right; you are only wanting to gain time by negotiations, and are meanwhile advancing and bombarding a defenceless city! What else do you want to conquer, when you are in possession of the capital? What is the good of our continuing our conversation if you act in this manner?"

Already one hears the roaring of the armies' motors. Cowering in three enormous garages, the chauffeurs sit in their huge machines, and pull the levers of the motors until they begin to whir, almost simultaneously, in three world cities. Which of the machines started that whirring a few hours earlier than the other two is of interest to-day only to a few patriotic historians, anxious to rehabilitate their own statesmen.

Have they read *Hamlet?* "There's nothing either good or bad, but thinking makes it so." . . .

*   *

Sazonov is calmer with the German Ambassador to-day, for yesterday there was a scene, protests, reconciliation, Russian embraces. *"Let's have done with that."* To-day: *"Further continuation of the Russian mobilisation-measures would force us to mobilise, and in that case a European war could scarcely be prevented."*

Sazonov: *"I will report to His Majesty."*

The German is followed by the Englishman, on whom Sazonov, reverting to Grey's proposal, urges haste.

Everywhere two races are being run. Europe's generals are spurring on the Ministers to run fast and reach the goal sooner than the enemy; Europe's Ministers are reining the generals back that they may not be run away with; for each of these mighty ones is at the same time horse and rider.

Sazonov laments the difficulty which he finds in restraining his General Staff; his plaint is telegraphed by the Tsar of all the Russias to the German Kaiser. The Kaiser heaves a sigh to the same effect (but hides it from his son); and the Premiers of all four countries were probably echoing it at the same hour. For if a horse has stood in its stall so long that it has almost forgotten how to run, then, when it is saddled and bridled at last and led to the stable door, already creaking on its hinges, it gives it a kick to force it open. But what has all that to do with peaceful folk outside, whose only ambition is to escape being ridden down?

To-day, then, the Petersburg Council of War confirms the official version of mobilisation against Austria, and the secret beginning of general mobilisation, the partial variety being *"technically impossible."*

Up to this point the motives of the participants have been susceptible to analysis and consideration; but here the conflict begins to degenerate into hysteria. From this moment onward only a partisan can distinguish the provoker from the provoked in Europe. The word "technical" was used then to frighten the Ministers into their corners, as it is used to-day to intimidate the historians. The brass hats propounded a theory of esoteric strategical lore, to be accepted in faith, not understood; and the laity murmured: *"Credo, quia absurdum est."*

* *

At the same time the Tsar, always anxious, like the Kaiser, to undo the effects of his energetic decisions, informs the German Ambassador that the decree of mobilisation does not constitute a hostile act against Germany. This message, for once, conceals no intrigue of the Generals; it is only the

Tsar's way of reassuring himself against his own fears. For the General dislikes the message, goes behind the Ambassador's back, and requests the presence of the German Military Attaché.

The German Major, whose invariable habit it was to appear in uniform, punctually to the minute, and to speak Russian, arrives to-day in mufti, an hour late, and says in French:

"We know for a fact that your mobilisation is proceeding."

"On my word of honour, you are wrong."

"I do not doubt it; but we have irrefutable proofs."

"Would you like my word of honour in writing?"

"No, thank you."

"In that case, I can only repeat to you: at this hour not one man and not one horse have been called up."

The Russian feels himself justified in this polite fiction, since the Tsar's ukase is still in his pocket (a staff officer, who was in the next room and heard the conversation, confirms the whole story, but with the charming variation that the ukase was actually *"lying on the table"*). The paper was signed by Nicholas and by the three Ministers of

War, Marine, and the Interior, and enacted *"general mobilisation."* The British Ambassador in Berlin stated in confirmation at the time that *"while the German Kaiser, at the Tsar's request, was working in Vienna . . . Russia mobilised."* It would be more accurate to say that while both Tsar and Kaiser alike wished to avoid mobilisation, Yanushkyevitch and Moltke alike were working for it. Nevertheless, it remains the fact that Russia had mobilised throughout her entire territory before any of the other Powers.

The victory of the Russian military party was, however, not yet complete; once more Wilhelm put a spoke in the wheel. In the evening the Tsar opened a new telegram from the Kaiser, containing a personal promise from the latter to secure peace if the Tsar would cancel mobilisation. The Tsar, strongly influenced by his impressionable, delicate wife, behind whom stood Rasputin, a foe to war, was delighted at the thought of having this instrument to use against the Generals. At 11 o'clock at night he rings up his Minister of War. Suchomlinov, deep in the work of mobilisation, hears the voice of his sovereign over the telephone. Nicholas reads him the telegram, but—there are two versions here—obviously could not make up his mind to give direct orders, only asking urgently:

"Is it, then, really impossible to hold up the mobilisation?"

"Impossible. One cannot put the brakes on and off mobilisation like a motor-car . . . perhaps Your Majesty will kindly ask for a report from the Chief of the General Staff."

A beautiful instance, this, of the way a War Minister's mind works. The disorganisation involved in reducing mobilisation to a smaller scale is more dreadful to him than war itself. We shall soon be able to note the same feelings in his German colleagues. Anxious moments. After a short time he is rung up again, this time by Yanushkyevitch, the Chief of the General Staff.

"Something frightful has happened! The Tsar has just rung up to say we are to reduce the general mobilisation to a partial one. I answered that it was technically impossible; but he insisted. The German Emperor has apparently put him on his honour. What shall I do?"

"Do nothing!"

"Thank God!"

Thus, in the night of July 29th/30th, the whole Russian Empire was *de facto* mobilised. How full are these nights of the ghostly voices of fear, of

lies, of Destiny sweeping through the brilliantly lit
Ministries in all capitals of the Continent!

The next morning the German Ambassador
calls on Sazonov. In what conditions would Russia cancel her mobilisation? A debate. Finally
the Minister writes down a form of words which
puts the Ultimatum in milder terms. This version
is sent to Berlin. It remains a formula; for in
Berlin they are by this time reckoning only with
numbers, not with degrees. The Minister drives
to his sovereign.

The Tsar's study in Peterhof. Tall windows
on the first floor, wide views over the Gulf of Finland, two tables with papers, a few war-pictures,
leather chairs—simplicity. Daily this room is
visited, as by an evil spirit, by Yanushkyevitch, the
right hand of Nicolai Nicholaevitch, the brutal
Grand Duke, the Tsar's uncle; Sazonov comes
only once a week. This afternoon, the afternoon
of the 30th, he stands before the Tsar and reads
the new telegram from the German Kaiser. If
Russia mobilises against Austria he cannot mediate. Sazonov replaces the telegram on the writing-
table.

*"We can no longer avoid war. Germany is ob-
viously withdrawing from her rôle as mediator,
and is only trying to gain time. In these circum-*

stances I do not think that Your Majesty ought to hesitate longer to issue the order for general mobilisation."

The Tsar, pale and with hesitating voice: *"Think of the responsibility which I take on myself if I follow your advice! Remember that it is a question of sending thousands and thousands of men to their deaths!"*

"Neither Your Majesty's conscience nor mine will have anything to answer for if war breaks out. Your Majesty and your Government will have done everything conceivable to spare the world this frightful ordeal. From now on we must think of the security of the Empire. The war will be breaking out at the hour which Germany has fixed!"

The Minister took *"a good hour"* to convince him.

Finally the Tsar said in a firm voice: *"Well, then, Sergius Dimitrievitch, telephone to the Chief of the General Staff that I give the order for general mobilisation."*

Sazonov bows, goes to the telephone in the antechamber, and passes the order to Yanushkyevitch. Then the Tsar signs the ukase for the Senate. The Chief of the General Staff, who foresees that his Imperial master will want to revoke his decision, remains inaccessible for the rest of the day, by agreement with Sazonov. At the same time the two arrange for the sequence of the mobilisations to be confused, and a false version sent to Paris and London.

*   *

One day before Russia took her military decision, England issued another warning and threat to both sides.

Benckendorff, *"with his natural eye for men and things,"* whose daily reports of Grey read like a bulletin on the moods of a great courtesan, feels the decision draw near. Lichnowsky has daily to defend Vienna's obstinacy, which he condemns himself, and to advise mediation in Petersburg when he cannot himself bring it about in Berlin.

But Vienna's repeated refusals have already made it easier for the British Cabinet to accomplish a change of front which it only half welcomed. Grey, who for five days had rejected the risk of possibly precipitating war by a threatening attitude towards one side or the other, while hoping to avert it by precisely such a threat, now sees in this dangerous method the only hope of salvation. In the same hour in which the Russian General in Petersburg is pointing to the clock and giving the

German Major his crafty *"word of honour,"* the
British Secretary of State is saying to the German
Ambassador in London:

*"The situation continues to grow more acute.
We can do nothing with Vienna. We have spoken
in friendly fashion, as always since you have been
here. I must not, however, deceive you. So long
as the conflict remains confined to Austria and
Russia, we can stand aside. But if Germany and
France should be involved, then the British Government would find itself forced to make up its
mind quickly."*

"I cannot say more," thinks Grey. "Perhaps
now they will believe it in Berlin." To make quite
certain, he had told Cambon an hour previously
that he was taking this step, but added: *"You
must not draw any final conclusions from our
orders to the Fleet. England is by no means entirely on the side of France to-day as she was in
the case of Morocco, for then you seemed to be
directly threatened by Germany. England has no
obligations. I must repeat this to you."*

On the same evening the Cabinets of Paris and
Petersburg, Berlin and Vienna, learn that England has taken up this attitude. Grey's warning
had a partial success with his allies, his threat a
partial success with his enemies. Paris, Peters-

burg, and Berlin feel uncertain enough to call a
halt; Vienna, however, in her inconceivable frivolity, remains resolute to cash the German blank
cheque in full.

*   *

Berlin is feeling less cheerful to-day; she sees
that things are growing grave; Russia is mobilising. Perplexity, blind to its own faults of omis-
sion, turns into wrath and is directed against
Vienna.

The most alarmed of all is the Kaiser. Had he
not come into line, and thus vetoed any possible
consequences of his earlier attitude? When he
reads in a report of the heavy responsibilities with
which Austria has burdened herself, he writes in
the margin: *"That is what worried me after reading the Serbian reply."* The report contains the
opinion that *"The Kaiser will give his ally Austria
the good advice not to overdraw the bow."* He
writes beside the words: *"These are phrases to
throw the responsibility on me. I refuse it!"* And
to the advice to submit the contested points to The
Hague Court of Arbitration he writes merely:
"Rubbish!" He has been of the same opinion on
that question for seven years.

In the evening he holds a Crown Council in

Potsdam.   Ministers and Generals sit at the table;
a decision is taken to mobilise in the event of general mobilisation in Russia, but it is not made public.   The Tsar's hint about The Hague is ignored,
for his own mobilisation had practically cut off
this way of escape.   But what is to be done with
England?   Patience.   On this evening Bethmann
will achieve his masterpiece.

The same night there arrives from London the
unambiguous warning which Berlin had refused to
believe when it came through its own Ambassador.
Panic, terror! True, after all! What's to be done?
Draw back?   Let the Kaiser wire with all speed
to the Tsar!   In the afternoon of July 30th the
telegram goes off, urgently advising peace.

Bethmann collapses.   He attempts to save, or to
divert on to other shoulders, what he can; he wires
to his Ambassador in Vienna: *"We are, of course,
ready to fulfil the obligation of our alliance, but
must decline to be drawn wantonly into a world
conflagration without having any regard paid to
our counsels."*   Under these words run the warning tones of Bismarck's ghostly voice: *"From the
moment in which Vienna becomes convinced that
the bridges between Germany and Russia are
burnt, Germany will be in danger of becoming to a
certain extent dependent on Austria, and finally*

NICHOLAS II

Czar of Russia

risking life and limb for Vienna's Balkan policy."
O, prophetic spirit! That is exactly what happened in July 1914.

Had the Chancellor wired his rebellion against Vienna four days earlier, Europe had been saved. To-day it was valueless, even if, as has been alleged, Tschirschky in Vienna purposely made no use of it.

For now the Army has taken over the reins in the Foreign Office; and for four whole years they will not let them go. The Generals telegraph: Moltke *"urgently advises"* immediate mobilisation of the whole army by Vienna; it sounds like the first word of command from Germany. Thousands more will follow it. So decisively does Germany's Commander-in-Chief intervene in the policy of alliances that Berchtold, when Conrad reads him the two columns from Berlin on the 31st, cries out: *"That is good! Who is in command, Moltke or Bethmann? I asked you to come here because I had the impression that Germany was wavering. Now, however, I have satisfactory explanations from authoritative military sources."* Only after this did Vienna *"decide to ask His Majesty to decree general mobilisation."* The old Emperor signed the edict, but how little he hoped from it and what his true feelings were is shown by a remark which he made during these days to Conrad von Hötzendorf: *"If the Monarchy is to go to hell now, at least it shall go like a gentleman."*

In Berlin that evening the Commanding General, Von Moltke, ordered the Chancellor to take back his decisive threat to Vienna: *"Please cancel order of instructions for the time"*; the only reason which Bethmann had proposed to give: *"since the General Staff just informs me that the military preparation (of Russia) will force us to a decision,"* was left out. Lerchenfeld tells us that Moltke *"had stated months previously that the moment was such a favourable one from the military point of view as might not recur for a considerable time"*; now a report from the Bavarian military plenipotentiary in Berlin confirms the fact that Moltke was *"bringing his influence to bear in order that the unusually favourable situation should be used to strike; he points out that France's military situation is nothing short of embarrassed, that Russia is anything but confident; moreover, the time of year is favourable, the harvest for the greater part already in, the annual training completed."*

This report from the Allied military expert shows what goes on in heads of this type; one may be sure that Yanushkyevitch in Petersburg and

Conrad in Vienna had used precisely the same words at precisely the same hour, even though we have no written record of them. The enemy is not confident, the harvest is in, the time of year favourable for operations. Strange that the heroes of these thoughts and decisions, all, without any exception, in all countries, succeeded in saving themselves from the hero's death!

At noon an "unnamed" source gave the official *Lokalanzeiger* a hint to publish the mobilisation decree, for which they had not yet succeeded in obtaining the Kaiser's signature, as an accomplished fact. At one o'clock a special edition of 100,000 copies appeared in Berlin. All diplomats wired it home. Jagow telephoned a *démenti* to the Embassies. No one believed him; the trick was unnecessary, for Petersburg had ordered mobilisation before the arrival of the false report from Berlin. The Tsar telegraphed again, asking for mediation. The Kaiser noted (July 30th): *"No! No, there is no thought of anything of that sort!! It is only a manœuvre to hold us back and increase the start they have already got. My work is at an end! W."*

"My work is at an end." Does not this echo the voice of his Generals? This is not a case of a man attempting to act with real statesmanship; that is, to put himself in the other man's place; to compare

the pressure put on the timid Tsar by his soldiers with the pressure put on the equally timid Kaiser, and to strengthen his cousin with a decisive word. After irritating Europe for twenty-five years with his speeches, for twenty-five days with his Nibelungen troth, without wanting war himself, the Kaiser, at the sight of his only really hated enemy, breaks out at last this evening with these words, which he notes on the last report from Petersburg: *"So the famous encircling of Germany has finally become a complete fact, despite every effort of our politicians and diplomats to prevent it. . . . A great achievement which arouses the admiration even of him who is to be destroyed as its result. Edward VII is stronger after his death than I am. I who am still alive. . . . And we walked into the net in the touching hope of thus pacifying England!!! All my warnings, all my pleas, were voiced for nothing. Now comes England's so-called gratitude for it! From the dilemma raised by our fidelity to the venerable old Emperor of Austria, we are brought into a situation which offers England the desired pretext for annihilating us. . . . This whole business must now be ruthlessly unmasked. And our Consuls in Turkey and India, agents, etc., must fire the whole Mohammedan world to fierce rebellion against this hated, lying, conscienceless nation of shop-keepers; for if we are bled to death, England shall at least lose India.*

"*W.*"

A torrent of genuine feelings, distorted ideas, resentments, and perfervid emotions mingles in these sentences, which anticipate the best catch-words of the next four years in Germany. How narrow—and yet what a passion of revenge, what a flame of genuine hatred, fostered by the monarch of one mighty Empire against another, because he felt himself looked down upon by his English uncle. When we see him, every whit as pessimistically as his ally in Vienna, beginning an undertaking from which one single "*No*" could have saved him, we cannot but ask what impelled him at last to venture it, in spite of all, against his better judgment: hate of England or fear of his Generals?

*   *

Bethmann's urgent command to secure acceptance of England's proposals reaches the German Ambassador in Vienna. Immediately, and even before the Berlin Generals can countermand it, the Ambassador invites himself to lunch with Count Berchtold. It is a question of hours, the destiny of Europe is at stake, and yet his dandiacal host insists that the Ambassador shall not present his message *"until they have left the table";* for gentlemen of this type never lose their appetites. Count Forgátch, also present, makes notes. Berchtold stands *"pale and silent";* he sees his indispensable war endangered at the very last moment! "What is the next thing to be done?" he asks himself. Why, change his clothes! For he wants to drive to the Emperor. Meanwhile, the German makes a last appeal to the conscience of the other Count. Forgátch, on the contrary, is in favour of a general mobilisation, for which Conrad proposes to get the Emperor's consent that evening. Berchtold is *"swayed this way and that by the most various influences."* Tisza is quoted. Unfortunately it is no longer possible to refuse altogether, so—but not until the next day—they agree, under the pressure from Berlin, to answer in set terms with a purely formal acceptance of Grey's mediation. They agree to *"approach"* the English proposals, letting the Serbian campaign, however, proceed meanwhile.

Even this was late; Count Berchtold held back this morsel of consent until it could do no harm. In Berlin the British Ambassador asked repeatedly and vainly for two whole days about the answer from Vienna. It was not sent to Berlin until twenty-four hours later, and was never transmitted to London from there. The Generals were in the saddle. Instead, general mobilisation was ordered in Vienna, a few hours later than in Petersburg.

For all that, the relations between the civil and military authorities in Vienna and in Berlin were very different. In Berlin, where the Generals were more efficient than the diplomats, the Generals ruled. In Vienna, where the reverse was the case, the skilled diplomats were able to give their orders to the Generals even after the outbreak of war. How they did it is shown by a telegram which was destined to be brought to light out of a hidden corner and exposed to the shuddering laughter of the later world. On the 28th General Potiorek, who had been sent out to conquer Serbia, and was destined to be beaten and sitting in Vienna again by Christmas, received a telegram to the effect that: *"Small skirmishes against Serbia are desirable, but engagements on a large scale which might result in failure would not be welcomed."*

In the capital, then, sits a Minister who has planned a war, but finds himself hindered by more powerful Ministers, sees a Conference for the purpose of avoiding his war looming nearer, and therefore has every interest in shooting quickly, so that his guns may impose silence on the statesmen. Accordingly, he wires to the front: *"Forward."* As, however, his confidence in his Generals is limited, he adds, "please, no engagements" (a euphemism for battles) "in which something undesirable might occur." Only a few strokes in the air, so as to be able to lie to Europe, and his allies in particular, and say the English step *"unfortunately came too late . . . hostilities having been already opened by Serbia."*

At the same time, however, Berchtold had also taken a step in Petersburg. Now he permitted his Ambassador to begin *"conversations"* with Sazonov, i.e. to talk over the Ultimatum, but not to discuss its *"justification."* Why did he do this now, after refusing for five days? Because now he was certain that Russia and Germany were definitely enemies; and now this minor Metternich could present Austria as peaceably inclined. The next days bring the proof.

*   *

In Berlin a *"state of danger of war"* is proclaimed at the same time (July 31st); an invention of the General Staffs, enabling them to mobilise before mobilisation in case of war. The military applaud Vienna's firm attitude. Berchtold's latest step in Petersburg is, indeed, known; and as it was

Austria and not Germany which had a quarrel with Russia, this should automatically have stopped the Germans too. But the Generals had the whip hand.

An hour later the British Ambassador made a last attempt at persuading Jagow to accept Grey's latest proposals.

Jagow: *"We have sent Russia an ultimatum with a grace of twelve hours."*

Goschen: *"Why then do you ask Russia to demobilise in the south also?"*

Jagow: *"To prevent her from alleging the pretext that her whole mobilisation was directed against Austria alone."*

The feeling in the Foreign Office in Berlin is described in a report from Count Lerchenfeld, which is summarised here: *"The Anglo-German proposals could quite well have been accepted in Vienna. . . . Months ago Moltke made the statement that, from a military point of view, times were more favourable than they were likely to be for an extremely long period to come. The reasons that he adduced were:*

1. *Superiority of the German artillery. France and Russia possess no howitzers.*
2. *Superiority of the German infantry rifle.*

3. *Wholly insufficient training of the French
   cavalry.*

*Social democrats, as in duty bound, have made de-
monstrations in favour of peace, but are now keeping very quiet. . . . The Kaiser, despite some
changes of mood, is now very serious and very
calm."*

In Petersburg they were quite as determined.
The German Ambassador drives to the Tsar in
Peterhof in the afternoon, and says:

*"I should like to describe to Your Majesty, quite
openly, the impression which the general Russian
mobilisation is bound to make in Germany. It will
be regarded not only as a threat and challenge to
Germany, but also as an insult to the German Kaiser, who is still attempting to mediate."*

The Tsar listens *"without moving a muscle
which might betray his inner feelings,"* then says:

"Do you really think so?"

Pourtalès: *"The only thing which could still
avert war would be cancellation of the edict of
mobilisation."*

The Tsar: *"You have been an officer yourself,
and must therefore know that it is technically impossible to suspend orders of that sort."* Thereupon he shows Pourtalès a telegram and an un-

finished letter to the German Kaiser. He does
not yet wholly admit defeat, for he sends a General
off to Berlin. This Russian Peace General never
reached Berlin, any more than Berchtold's long-
delayed acceptance from Vienna ever reached
London.

As Germany simultaneously made the question
of peace or war depend on cancellation of the Russian mobilisation, it may be noted as a fact that
things came to war because no one can suspend a
mobilisation *"without a mishap."*

At midnight on the following day Count Pourtalès presented the German Ultimatum. Sazonov
asked:

*"Why are you not satisfied with the Tsar's word
of honour to the German Kaiser?"*

*"Because it held only as long as there still re-
mained a prospect of composing the Austro-Rus-
sian quarrel on account of Serbia. Can you give
me a guarantee that Russia intends to keep the
peace even in the event that agreement with Austria is not reached?"*

*"I am unable to give you an affirmative answer
to that question."*

*"In that case, you cannot blame us for an un-
willingness to allow Russia a longer start in mobilisation."*

This last point is confirmed by the Serbian Minister, who wired home from Petersburg at the same hour that: *"Russia appears to be spurning all the negotiations with the purpose of gaining time for the concentration of her Army. When she is ready, she will declare war on Austria."*

Only the last sentence proved incorrect. For a few hours before that menacing conversation, Sazonov had an extremely friendly talk with the Austro-Hungarian Ambassador:

"We shall not stir so long as conversations with a view to understanding are in progress. Besides, you mobilised first."

The Hungarian protests vehemently. Sazonov ends the schoolboys' argument with this memorable piece of irony: *"Enough of this chronology!"* Thereupon they discuss the Ultimatum, as they had done five days previously. At the close of the conversation Sazonov declares himself much relieved.

*   *

On July 31st, even before the Ultimatum had been presented in Petersburg, the Kaiser made his first war speech from the balcony of the Palace in Berlin, a speech in which he dealt with the Sword, God, and the Enemy.

Meanwhile, the technical question of how to word the declaration of war was causing some difficulty. Two declarations were written out, for all eventualities (one in advance for France); but it was like Faust with his translation of the Bible. The first proposal was to write: *"Accepter la guerre octroyée."* That, however, would not do, for on consulting the dictionary, it was found that this might mean that the war was "approved." Then some phrases about compulsion were introduced, but these again had to be scratched out. Finally, the reason for the war was ignored and this formula was adapted: *"relève le défi"*: accept the challenge.

At 1 P.M. it was telegraphed to the Ambassador, to be presented at five. At two o'clock a fresh telegram from the Tsar suddenly arrived in Berlin. At the time, however, no one thought of wiring as a first step to the Ambassador, bidding him hold up the declaration of war till further orders, although the Tsar's most sensible telegram ran:

"I understand that you are obliged to mobilise, but I wish to have the same guarantee from you that I gave you, that these measures do not mean war and that we shall continue negotiating."

Nevertheless, Jagow and Zimmermann drive to the Palace to stop the mobilisation. Although unsuccessful in this all-important point, the one remains two years longer in office, the other three.

At five o'clock in the afternoon cars come tearing down the Linden from the Palace; officers stand up in them, wave handkerchiefs, and shout through their cupped hands: *"Mobilisation!"* The crowd cheers, and swarms round them.

Only in the Palace itself, in the shadow of the royal wings, everything proceeds with Prussian discipline. The report says: *"At the Kaiser's orders a policeman stepped before the gate of the Palace, shortly after five o'clock, and informed the waiting crowd that the decision to mobilise had been taken. The crowd, deeply moved, struck up the hymn, 'Now thank we all our God.'"*

*   *

The Foreign Office had sent the declaration of war to the Ambassador in Petersburg, not only in French but also in two alternative forms in cipher, according to whether the enemy returned a refusal or no answer at all. The Ambassador had thus nothing to do beyond carrying the message.

It took some five minutes to write out the Note after decoding it. Count Pourtalès did not trouble to copy the whole twice, but *"time being short"* put the paper bearing both versions in his pocket and drove off to Sazonov (August 1st).

"After asking M. Sazonov three successive times whether he could make me the declaration demanded at our last conversation . . . I handed over the Note as instructed."

When he was gone, the Russian read the double declaration of war from Germany:

"Russia, having refused to accede to this demand, having believed it unnecessary to respond to this demand, and having made it manifest by this* refusal / attitude *that her action was directed against Germany, I have the honour, on behalf of my Government, to inform Your Excellency as follows:*

"His Majesty the Kaiser, my august Sovereign, accepts this challenge in the name of the Empire."

So adroit was Count Pourtalès.

After midnight the Tsar at Peterhof suddenly receives a fresh telegram from the German Kaiser wanting to avert war at the last moment; handed in at Berlin three hours before the presentation of the declaration of war and containing an urgent warning against even the slightest violation of the frontier, it thus suspended the declaration of war. Signature, *Willi.*

A last of last hopes awakes in the Tsar. He thinks:

"That is a sort of revocation of the declaration of war; at the very least, it makes it only conditional. Yesterday I sent my adjutant to Berlin. If I stop the troops on the frontier, it may all come right yet." Instantly he telephones to Sazonov and orders him to ring up the German Ambassador at once.

It is close on four in the morning. Count Pourtalès has spent the whole night packing. When the telephone rings now, he thinks it is a ghost he hears. What? Is that really the Prime Minister on whom he has just declared war? *What* has the Tsar received? A fresh telegram from the Kaiser? My God! Sazonov carefully repeats the exact words, with the hour of despatch of the Berlin telegram; then he asks:

"How am I to reconcile this telegram with your declaration of war?"

Once more Reason creeps into the circle of weak or criminal diplomats; one last time. With what words will she inspire the German Count? Will he not call into the mouthpiece *"I'm coming,"* call for his hat and his car, hurry down to receive his Sovereign's invaluable telegram, or at least a copy of it, before five minutes are past?

Nothing of the sort. He is a diplomat—that is to say, he has learned the correct thing to do when one has declared war. And Sazonov, waiting on the telephone, hears only these words (recorded in Pourtalès' own memoirs):

"I regret that I can give no information on this point. The telegram may perhaps be earlier than that in which I was instructed to present the declaration in question. Further, I must request you to apply to the American Chargé d'Affaires, who has taken charge of our interests. In four hours we shall be leaving." And rings off.

"Perhaps." "Declaration in question." "Further, I must request." Coldness, superficiality, the desire to avoid complications; the typical attitude of a European diplomat. But after the war had been lost, the noble Count was neither held up to the ridicule of his nation for his *"double"* declaration of war, nor made to answer for his rejection of the Imperial telegram.

CHAPTER XI

THE NEUTRALS

THE Balkans are a massive mountain chain, as threatening and as savage as their name implies; and even as their glittering quartz is broken by dull grey volcanic rock, so the twenty-five million inhabitants of the peninsula wear a veneer of Western civilisation over their passionate natures. The West sought to dupe them with its sciences and arts, but they in return shocked the peoples of Europe with their Asiatic ways, rolling down into the plains like lava from their volcanoes. What do we care for Serbian comitadjis fighting against the Bulgarian Tsar, for cities whose very names our tongues can scarcely get round? For the duel between two dynasties in Serbia and their struggle with Greeks and Albanians for a Macedonia which has laid dark and almost unknown since the days of Alexander the Great? For the hospodars of Wallachia, and the intrigues of their successors between Russia and Turkey, for Bes-

sarabia? Of what value to us are the subterranean
ways of the last sultans, who by poison and dag-
ger built up a sovereignty on the heaped corpses
of whole nations, and left a tradition of murder and
brigandage behind them? *"Not worth the bones of
a Pomeranian Grenadier."*

At first they were too crafty to make a decision.
All five Balkan countries remained neutral during
the first months or years.

*　　　*

Roumania had secretly, long before, joined the
Triple Alliance; but it was soon to be seen how that
Quadruple Alliance remained in practice a Dual
Alliance. When Count Czernin, the new Austrian Minister, proposed, a year before the war, that
the secret treaty should be submitted to the Chamber, the old King of Roumania was terrified. Weak
(like the other European kings) but at bottom
honourable, a Hohenzollern, Adjutant to the
Crown Prince Frederick in the Danish War, husband of a princess who wrote poetry, always nearer
in spirit to the decent and, therefore, powerless
peasantry of his alien land than to the Balkan at-
torneys who ruled it—this King Carol let the two
parties alternately dip into the lucky-bag, and,
consequently, had dreaded nothing more em-

phatically than an open alliance with either side.

And yet even the Liberals—Parisian blend—
who had been ruling since the end of 1913, were to
be won if they were given Transylvania, in which
millions of Roumanians had been for centuries
subject to the Magyars. At that time they offered
a more or less loose adherence to the Monarchy—
very much on the lines of Franz Ferdinand's ideas;
but Tisza refused, and the old Emperor was the
more strongly against it because his nephew was
for it. The murder of the Archduke, therefore,
made a particularly deep impression in Bucharest;
they saw a friend of Roumania go down.

Vienna's Ultimatum to Serbia transformed these
feelings *in a few hours.* They had just won
victories at Serbia's side; they thought Austria
must be mad to start a war whose tangles offered
a prospect of seeing Roumania's old claims to
Transylvania more easily satisfied by neutrality
than by alliance. The Balkan King with the German heart did not let the Austrian Minister read
the Ultimatum through to the end, but interrupted, aghast: *"That means a world war!"* And
it was long before he could collect his thoughts and
decide on his policy. He felt his secret alliance
to be suspended in a vacuum; and when, a few
days later, the Austrian appealed to his honour,

saying that he must come in, a treaty was a treaty
—the old King collapsed across his desk in bitter
tears and tried to tear the *Pour le Mérite* from his
neck.

Meanwhile the German Kaiser telegraphed to
Bucharest *"as a Hohenzollern"* in an almost
threatening tone. Result—a Crown Council. The
King proposed helping Austria, according to
treaty; only one man, Peter Carp, voted for it. All
the rest denied the *casus fœderis,* since Vienna had
taken steps in Belgrade without previous consultation. The real cause of the opposition was, however, Hungary; for why should they help their mortal enemy out of her straits? The King gave at least
the assurance that Austria could leave her Roumanian frontier unguarded: *"So long as I am
King, Roumania shall never take the field against
Austria!"*

Bratianu, however, the Premier—a man of
French sympathies and education—reflected that
old gentlemen do not live for ever, and, at all
events, ordered new cannon—from Krupp's, of
course.

*   *

Bulgaria felt her hatred of Serbia and her hostility to Russia since her last visit to the Tsar's

Court, together with her lost war, drawing her to the German side: she would go over to the Triple Alliance if it guaranteed her the territories she had lost. Yet she was to hesitate a year before binding herself. Montenegro, however, which was Serbian by race but hated Serbia, soon gave up her shadow-game; the King of the Black Mountains had long been buying up Russian bonds in Paris and Vienna, and so hastened *"passionately"* to the help of his struggling brothers, Russia's allies. Did he believe that his Army could keep up the value of the Russian bonds—or did he believe in the Russian bonds and sacrifice his Army to them? He was to end by losing all—money, war, and land.

The Queen of Greece had been the guest of her Imperial brother in Berlin in July. He urged her to join the Triple Alliance, backing his argument with reference to an (as yet non-existent) Turco-Bulgarian alliance with Germany. Constantine refused to support Bulgaria, his enemy of yesterday: *"In this case I would not take the side of Austria against the Slavs, as it is said in Your Majesty's telegram."* This first reaction of the King's was truly Greek in its unambiguity.

The Kaiser is furious; but since the imperious tone proves useless, he adopts the moral: *"I feel that it goes without saying that the mere memory of your father, who fell by the hand of a murderer, will keep you and Greece from taking the part of the Serbian assassins."* Should this not prove to be the case, Constantine is threatened with an immediate attack from three allies, together with the rupture of all personal relations, and that at a moment when the Kaiser's sister is still in Berlin. The King, unalarmed, wires back that he is remaining neutral.

In Constantinople—as in London and Washington—the Germans were well represented; Wangenheim and Lichnowsky alone warned their blinded superiors in July 1914; while Bernsdorff, in 1916, stood up even to Ludendorff, the dilettante dictator. Freiherr von Wangenheim declared against alliance with Turkey. He was a brilliant figure, highly gifted, light of touch, pleasant, adroit, a friend of the arts and versed in women: in every respect the opposite of the typical German diplomat. Urged now by Berlin to persuade Turkey into a treaty, this statesman answers with irrefutable arguments: The Minister of War has offered him an alliance, he had evaded committing himself. The Kaiser, in the margin: *"Nonsense. Let him first join them to us, the rest will be taken care of!"*

This single note by the Kaiser, scribbled in a

hasty moment, without consultation with others—
just as in the days of Louis XIV—decided the
whole Turkish question. Wangenheim took it as
a "*peremptory order*" and, against his better judgment, concluded an alliance which was in the ultimate issue to prove fatal for both parties. As
though with prophetic insight, it was concluded for
four years, and ran out at exactly the same time as
did the failing strength of the two contracting
parties.

*   *

For years past Italy had been a member of the
Triple Alliance only on paper—paper which was
yellowing in three locked safes, unknown to almost everybody. She had reached an understanding with Russia and France; and there was only
one State which the Italian nation hated—its ally
Austria. The latter had, therefore, need of re-
doubled caution did she wish to make sure of her
ally's support before embarking on adventure.
Vienna had, indeed, asked Rome a year previously
if she might go to war with Serbia, but had then
received the same veto from Rome as from Berlin.
San Giuliano, Italy's old and cautious statesman,
had, like Giolitti, uttered a warning against this
"*periculosissima aventura.*"

"Well, then, this time we'll do it off our own bat," thought the War Counts in Vienna. But all Metternich's arts, as transmitted in dozens of instructions to the Ambassadors, were lost on Rome's subtlety; and even before the Ultimatum was put on paper the Italian Minister was opposing it. He told the German Ambassador that in the opinion of his legal advisers no Government, neither the Serbian nor another, could be made responsible for political agitation. Italy could not, therefore, consent to be an accomplice if Austria should propose to take action against Serbia. The German Secretary of State himself admitted that the *casus fœderis* had not arisen for Italy in the Serbian conflict.

The German Ambassador in Rome, Von Flotow —a clear-sighted man, but left by Berlin in the dark—uttered his warnings from the first; while the Austrian, Von Mérey, of delicate health, but self-willed and obstinate, hindered any step which might have won over his country's ally. This scene, with all its alternations, was played for the most part outside Rome, in the watering-places where Ministers and Diplomats go in summer as a cure for their gout. It was so managed, however, that the Ministers always escaped in their cars to Rome when they feared *démarches,* and had van-

ished from it again when the Diplomats arrived in
pursuit.

So Vienna failed even in her attempt to be at
least polite at the last moment. It was like a scene
on the films. The Austrian followed the Foreign
Minister to Rome in order to inform him of the Ultimatum to Serbia a day before its presentation.
The Minister was unable to receive him, and left
Rome. Then the Austrian fell ill, and his guile-
less Councillor of Embassy caught the Minister at
the seaside on the following day, when the latter
was long since in possession of the whole story.

In point of fact, there was nothing more to be
done. Both Salandra, the Premier, and San Giuliano, the Foreign Minister, the latter an old friend
of Germany, the former an intriguer, declared:
"Italy is neutral, because the Triple Alliance is
defensive, whereas Vienna is taking the offensive
against Belgrade; incidentally, under Article VII
of the Treaty, we can claim compensation for any
conquests to strengthen Austria in the Balkans."

In no point did the German Government show
itself more insistent or more sensible than in the
messages which it sent daily to Vienna, urging it
to offer Italy something quickly in order to ensure
her support. In no point did Vienna show itself
more greedy and more shortsighted. Von Flotow

was so urgent that at last, on his own responsibility, he suggested Valona—only to receive a contemptuous refusal. Von Mérey, on the other hand, gave his advice with growing vehemence against any offer, as tending only to increase Italy's demands; rising at last to these heights: *"That would be like calling to a friend who had fallen into the Danube: 'I am not going to pull you out; but if you get out by yourself, you must give me compensation.'"*

When Von Mérey plunged into the raging torrent of this simile, no one helped *him* out. He failed to perceive that it was Austria who had insisted on leaping into the Danube, and now, as she was gliding rapidly towards Belgrade, called back cheerful assurances of her perfect contentment. At such games only the Nibelungen can preserve their patience. Herr von Mérey, however, is in such joyous mood that he asks permission to say in Rome: *"If Italy does not carry out her duty under the Alliance to the last man, we too shall hold ourselves released in toto from our obligations, and shall consider Italy as having left the Triple Alliance."*

Count Berchtold really deserves praise for not having approved this ludicrous proposal from his Ambassador. He saw in his mind's eye the Roman legal experts, after such a threat from their ally, wrap themselves in their robes and cry like Wotan: *"Go, I cannot hold thee!"* He suggested compensation if Austria, with Italy's support, made any conquests in the Balkans.

This offer was, however far too small, and came far too late; for in the meantime England's decision had matured, and the peninsula, with its small fleet and undefended coastline, could not possibly venture on a naval war against the chief naval Power. San Giuliano accordingly demanded pledges for his neutrality. Finally he let drop the name Trentino, whereupon Von Mérey interrupted the conversation with these words:

"If ever in the course of our discussions during the past years I have shown an undiplomatic bluntness, I will now make good this error by refraining from returning à sottise *in answer to your inadmissible suggestions."*

With this phrase, which might come from the third act of a tragedy by Dumas, the Austrian statesman dismissed Italy, whom he was supposed to be courting, stepped politely back, and allowed her to throw herself into his rival's arms.

*   *

When, however, the Kaiser Wilhelm read Victor

Emanuel's evasive telegram, not only did he write
on the margin: *"Scoundrel! Insolence!"*; but a
true light broke on him, and with real understanding he noted: *"Our Allies are dropping away from
us like rotten apples even before war breaks out.
A total collapse of both German and Austrian
diplomacy. This should and could have been
avoided."* Never was Wilhelm II's vision clearer
or his words juster.

*   *

When that vast crowd, fired by Jaurès' historical
speech, thronged through the streets of Brussels
shouting *"Down with war!"* the German Minister
reported this to Berlin, with the addition: *"A
speech the reproduction of which would be su-
perfluous."*

Yesterday this Herr von Below had received
by courier a mysterious envelope, with the order
not to open it until receipt of telegraphic orders.
In reality the Germans—sympathetic judges who
do not pronounce the death-sentence until immediately before its execution—did not leave the
delinquent long in terrified uncertainty. He had
long suspected this. For years Count von Schlieffen's plan, which held victory over France to be
obtainable only by marching through Belgium,

had been considered quite possible by Belgium's leaders, though always denied by the Germans.

Three years previously Bethmann had denied it in the Reichstag; Jagow, fifteen months ago, in the Foreign Affairs Committee; but when the Belgian Royal couple had paid their inaugural visit, the Emperor had at table made a *"jesting"* reference to the matter of such a nature that the Secretary of State had still been trying in vain at the very railway-station to efface the impression from the minds of the startled sovereigns.

This incident, combined with the construction of strategic railways in Germany and the discoveries of French agents, had so increased the fear of a German invasion that the General Staff in Brussels made arrangements with the British Military Attaché, in the event of a German attack, to give a British expeditionary force all necessary information concerning roads, supplies, munitions, etc. No treaty was concluded, there were no ministerial negotiations, the documents repeatedly contain the phrase: *"Only if the Germans invade."* The fact that no mention is made of the possibility of a French invasion is no immediate proof of France's virtue, but only of Belgium's confidence in France.

For two generations it had been the other way

round. In order to prevent the conquest of Belgium by Louis Philippe, Prussia had proposed to the other four Great Powers to guarantee its perpetual neutrality, after the Swiss model. The kingdom was based on this neutralisation. Prussia was thus the first of the five godfathers at Belgium's cradle. A pattern of modern harmony, this treaty; firstly, as a voluntary declaration on oath of the inviolability of a coveted maiden; secondly, as a model for the United States of Europe, which means nothing more than an extension of the principle of neutralised states; thirdly, as an example of the unification of two nations of almost equal strength in a common *ménage* in the heart of nationalist Europe. To crown all, the most democratic constitution of its age was that of Belgium itself.

But what, after all, is the most solemn of treaties but a scrap of paper, to be torn up when interests change? Such was the view of Napoleon III, who wanted to take Belgium, and suggested to Bismarck recognition of the Norddeutscher Bund in return for his support in conquering Belgium. Bismarck refused, but kept France's incautious letter and sent it to England, whose neutrality he needed, when he began his subsequent campaign.

At Sedan part of the besieged army could have escaped into Belgium, but the frontier was closed, and Napoleon lost his throne through the closed barrier of the land with whose banners he had thought to adorn it.

When, however, at the beginning of that war, the Belgian Minister had asked for a renewal of the guarantee of neutrality, Bismarck had replied with no phrases about the protection of small nations or sworn treaties, but only with these undramatic words: *"I am surprised that a man of your acumen should think I could be so simple as to throw Belgium into France's arms."*

To-day this was the clear purpose of the sealed letter to the German Minister. (Amid all the tragic circumstances occurred the comic one, that the head of the Belgian section in the Berlin Foreign Office was on leave, and had locked up his desk with the papers in it, leaving the Diplomats standing helpless before this drawerful of mysteries!)

London had sent simultaneous questions to Berlin and Paris about Belgium. Paris promised to observe the treaty. Jagow evaded the question, saying that his answer would betray Germany's strategic plans. Courtly old M. Davignon, the Foreign Minister in Brussels, nods; he sees here

confirmation of his old suspicions. He sends a
gentleman over to the German Minister to give
him a hint. The messenger repeats to the German
England's question and France's reply, adding
that the Frenchman proposes to publish his declaration officially, through to-day's Brussels Press.
Thereupon Von Below sits up in his chair, looks—
according to the report—at the ceiling with half-
closed eyes, and repeats all that has been said with
phonographic accuracy. Then he expresses his
thanks to the Minister, offers his visitor a cigarette
to mark the close of the official conversation, and
says in a wholly altered voice: *"I am quite convinced that Belgium has nothing to fear from
Germany. We shall certainly give the same declaration."*

Embarrassment in palace, ministry, and capital;
the whole land quakes as before a coming tempest.
Aghast they wonder: "How could we leave the
siege guns which we ordered from Krupp lying
there in store, long after they were ready, merely
because our earthworks were not finished. What
folly!"

King Albert, quiet, cautious, intelligent, a Hohenzollern on his mother's side, interested in naval
construction, Alpine climbing, travelling, and the
Congo, with leanings towards modern art, Saint-

Saëns, César Franck; the Queen, beautiful, like many Bavarian Princesses, daughter of the venerable Duke Karl Theodor, who became a doctor out of inclination, and restored the eyesight of thousands of poor creatures out of humanity—this marriage, in which three out of the four parents are German, is marked by gentle breeding, reserve, and that mixture of Gallic and Germanic culture which history and geographical situation make usual in Belgium. Now the King writes a very loyal and intimate letter in German to the Kaiser, reminding him of his repeated assurances.

On the following morning the German Minister speaks to the Belgian Government and the Press in the same tone as on the previous day. At three o'clock his words appear in the *Soir*: *"Your neighbour's roof may perhaps burn, but your own house will be safe."*

When diplomats try to be poetic, some mischance usually occurs. All Brussels clings to this sentence; three hours later every child in the little country knows it. Simultaneously comes the news: Germany has invaded Luxemburg! Brussels breathes again; so much the safer our own front!

Suddenly, towards evening, Below appears at the Ministry. Three hours previously he had received orders to open the secret message. He read it without surprise. He was ordered to represent his ultimatum as though just received—drives over, presents his Note.

The Belgian reads: As we have reliable information that the French advance along the Meuse *"leaves no doubt"* of her intention to march through Belgian territory, and as we fear that Belgium will be unable to resist without assistance, Germany is threatened and must in self-preservation anticipate the attack, and therefore must *"herself also enter upon Belgian soil."* If Belgium preserves benevolent neutrality, she is promised territorial aggrandisement at the expense of France. If she maintains a friendly attitude Germany will pay for her troops and make damage good; if she is hostile, war. Twenty-four hours to decide.

The Belgian, still astounded at tone and pretext, is silent. Then he says in rising wrath: *"We expected anything but this, Your Excellency! Germany, who pretended to be our friend, and now expects us to play such a miserable part!"*

The Ministerial Council unanimously resolves to refuse. During the evening and the night there are meetings in the palace, till 4 A.M. At half-past one in the morning the German Minister comes to the Belgian Foreign Office to say:

"French dirigibles have thrown bombs, cavalry has crossed the frontier, although war has not been declared."

"Where did these incidents take place, Your Excellency?"

"In Germany, Baron."

"In that case I cannot understand why you come here at night to report them in Brussels."

"That you may see that these acts, which are contrary to international law, are calculated to lead to the supposition that other acts, contrary to international law, will be committed by France."

This grotesque nocturne is the last official act but one of the German Minister in Brussels. An hour later the Frenchman rings up the Ministry: *"Moving lights in the sky! Undoubtedly German dirigibles!"* The Frenchman is over-excited; they are stars, but every soul that night believes that they are moving. France offers armed assistance. It is declined with thanks; diplomatic assistance only is asked, in order to give Germany no pretext. A wire for *"intervention"* is also sent to England.

Meanwhile the German Ultimatum has expired at 7 A.M. Not till twenty-three hours later does the German Minister declare that Germany *"will if necessary take measures by force of arms."* Three hours later the first German troops come under the fire of Belgian gendarmes at Gemmenich.

At the same time the German Minister receives a note point-blank, his sovereign, simultaneously, a long range shot by wire. The first runs: *"I have the honour to inform Your Excellency that from to-day the Belgian Government are unable to recognise your diplomatic status, and cease to have official relations with you."* The King wires to the Kaiser in French; his tone is irreproachable:

"The feelings of friendship which I have expressed to Your Majesty and those of which you have so often assured me . . . did not permit me to assume for a single moment that Your Majesty would force us, in the face of all Europe, to the cruel choice between war and dishonour, between fidelity to treaties and faithlessness to our international obligations. Albert."

CHAPTER XII

THE treaty system of old Europe was built on a morass. Each lured the other on, watched till at last he touched the forbidden fruit, then cried: "The robber has violated the legal frontier; help!" As Christian morality forbade any aggression, self-defence alone could be shown as the motive; and therefore each group waited for aggression from the enemy, to enforce the *casus fœderis*. What profoundly ironical truth, when the Prussian Minister in Munich, questioned respecting the *casus fœderis,* wrote: *"The small number of persons who are familiar with the treaty appear to interpret it differently."*

But even apart from alliances, the peoples themselves, and above all the lowest classes, who had to fight and suffer the war in all its reality, could be roused only by the conviction that they were victims of aggression. So each sought to construe the other's conduct as such. They might have stood under arms for weeks, confronting one another, and given the watching world time to speak the decisive word of unarmed reason.

But the will of the Generals leaped across like an invisible spark from the recesses of their palaces in the Capitals to the front posts, where already men were stamping impatiently, eager to open the drama. Everywhere there were patrols of from five to twenty men prowling along the frontiers. A certain number of the *"frontier violations,"* on which most of the declarations of war based their *"casus fœderis,"* were therefore genuine; what was invented sounded plausible, and might become truth an hour later. It is an idle waste of time to decide the conflict of those documents, with which each side sought after the event to prove its own innocence. The only important things are the intentions of the leaders behind, the levity of the advance posts in front, and the ambiguity of the treaties which reckoned on both these things. "There's nothing either good or bad, but thinking makes it so."

Every General Staff in Europe now discovered frontier violations, to work on the hesitating diplomats at home. According to Berchtold's fantasies, Serbian ships had fired on Austrian troops, while the German General Staff credited itself with a

Russian invasion at Johannisburg. *"With this action Russia has opened war against us,"* the relieved diplomats informed the Press. A subaltern officer had, in fact, crossed the frontier, in ignorance of the German declaration of war, which had already been despatched.

It was more important for France to be the victim of aggression; not only the Socialists, but also their enemies the French bankers, were disinclined to chime in with the Tsar's hymn; the view of the all-important ally, England, depended entirely on whether or not France were attacked. Isvolski, the unscrupulous abettor of the War Party in Paris, wired many messages which were afterwards revealed by the Russian Revolution. The French Minister of War is said to have cynically confided to his Military Attaché: *"We can say easily enough that we are ready in the supreme interest of peace to retard mobilisation for the time; that need not stop us from continuing and even intensifying our preparations; only large movements of troops should, if possible, be avoided."* When the Germans really came, Isvolski wired in triumph to his chief:

"The Germans are crossing the frontier in small detachments. This makes it possible for the Government to tell the Chamber that France is being

© August Scherl

MAJOR GENERAL COUNT VON MOLTKE

Chief of Staff of the Imperial Army, 1914–1916

attacked. The German invasion of Luxemburg is looked on very favourably here, for it will inevitably evoke a protest from England and incite her to act. Even more effective for England would be the violation of Belgium, which is expected here." A diabolical document, which reveals the cynicism of these circles in Europe! At the same time, Paris announced the following places as scenes of German attacks: Longwy, Cirey, Delle (near Belfort).

The Germans were out of luck in this respect. They made the same assertions, but were able to speak only of *"various points," "German localities,"* of an attempt to destroy the railway lines at Wesel and at Kochem in the Palatinate; they actually fell back on carrier-pigeons flying over the frontier at Basle, and on French officers in disguise said to have crossed the frontier in motor-cars at Walbeck. The motor-cars, especially, one of which was alleged to have been stopped but afterwards to have turned back into Holland, were represented in London as *"the worst conceivable"* violation of neutrality. Bombs said to have been dropped at the same time on the railway line near Nuremberg were afterwards denied. To prove the existence of the *casus fœderis,* it was reported to Rome that doctors had infected wells near Metz with cholera bacilli. Such reports presented a picture of August 1st unsurpassed by any poet's imagination, and in the general terror projected outward by the great searchlights, searching Heaven and Earth for enemies, only the Director of Police in Stuttgart preserved his sense of humour, reporting: *"Clouds are taken for aviators, stars for dirigibles, bicycle-spokes for bombs."*

Another path stood open. By the utmost caution, and by restriction of the German mobilisation to the East, the powerful anti-war elements in Paris might be strengthened, France's entry into the war delayed. France, alone of the countries in danger, had, under pressure from her Socialists, withdrawn her troops ten kilometres from the frontier; but this was done principally in the hope of influencing England's decision.

*   *

In Paris the German Ambassador had confined himself to the part of a postman, except that he opened the *"notes as ordered"* before handing them in. His obligato question as to France's neutrality received the obligato reply that she would act *"as her interests dictated"*—a phrase containing a neat double meaning, when the "interest" on the many millions lent to Russia is remembered. When

Viviani next day described the Ambassador's procedure as "extraordinary" and his question as "a threat," and expected him to ask for his passports at last, the latter merely answered: *"I have packed up."*

The same day Cambon wired to Paris from Berlin that as telegraphic communications were interrupted he must act independently, but did not propose to ask for his passports, but rather to wait till he was thrown out. Both Ambassadors acted logically as the nature of their alliances demanded; each wished to be assaulted in order to be able to call for help.

Meanwhile mobilisation began—at 3:40 P.M. in Paris, at 5 P.M. in Berlin. Here is another problem over which the nations afterwards disputed, long and jealously, each wanting to be the last. As, however, organisation is everything in this matter, the finger of the clock but little, we may repeat Sazonov's ironical remark: *"Enough of this chronology!"*

While the German Embassy in France was making ready to be off, a wire arrived from Berlin. It contained Germany's astonishing offer to France: If she remained neutral she should not be attacked, but the fortresses of Toul and Verdun must be occupied for security's sake. If you

promise not to fall on me during my duel with
your friend, I must ask you first to hand over your
gun, as reward for this attitude.

This offer was, however, never made. It would
have given Delcassé the one weapon still lacking in
his armoury; and soon after, when the Cabinet was
reconstructed, he took the portfolio of Foreign
Affairs, which was fittingly his in a war with Germany.

At last someone had to take the first step, and
this someone was neither Moltke nor Pau, neither
Castelnau nor Tirpitz, but an insignificant general
in Berlin, really doing policeman's work, but bearing the imposing title of "Commander in Chief in
the Marks." This functionary informed the
Foreign Office briefly that he was compelled *"in
view of the authenticated frontier violations, to
employ the same measures in connection with the
French Legation and the French generally, as
have already been made use of towards the Russian
Legation and the Russians."* On this even Jagow
took his red pencil and wrote on the margin:
*"What sort of measures are these? We are not yet
at war. Diplomats are still accredited."*

For this declaration of war, too, was hard to
draw up: they did not like to base it on France's
evasive answer, so resorted to the violated frontier

and the Nuremberg bombs. But this was too much for the long-suffering wire between Berlin and Paris; it refused to transmit that declaration of war, and when the Ambassador at the other end tried to read the telegram, the groups were all mixed up.

Herr von Schön had, however, gathered that the telegram dealt with the declaration of war. He therefore construed it as well as he could himself; and in the afternoon gave M. Viviani various grounds for war, including the Nuremberg bombs, which *had* remained legible, but of which the Prussian Minister in Munich had wired a denial to Berlin, shortly after despatch of the telegram.

On this grotesque basis the "Franco-German War" began.

*   *

Britannia still held the balance in her hand, but her eyes were not bound; they looked across to the Continent through the strongest of glasses to see where hope blossomed most greenly.

The Pan-Germans, the civilians at any rate, had a classical conception of England: *"A small German force is enough to stop the mouths of the heroes across the Channel for good and all. . . . We only have to throw across a division, and England is settled."* The Berlin diplomats had their own views: "Crafty, jealous, but pretty far away across the water, and its few thousand mercenaries won't so much as have landed before we are in Paris. The sort of people, too, who want to make money out of everything, so will remain neutral, if only on that account." Even at the last moment, however, when Grey sent word that Vienna and Petersburg must demobilise at once, or all was lost, Zimmermann merely thought that Lichnowsky was guarding himself with his warnings against being caught out like Pourtalès, and wanted to wave England's pacification before the Kaiser at the last moment, in order to make himself out a great statesman and slip into Bethmann's shoes. Lichnowsky, whose enemies within his own Embassy bandied such stories about, heard of them, and said: "That shot comes from *Stumm!*" The Generals were more sceptical. Schlieffen himself had taught them to count on England coming in. The Kaiser's shortsighted eyes had been clouded with hate, but in this case he saw clear again, as though a cataract had been removed. His personal friends in the Navy and the Colonies urged him to find some way to get on terms with the British dynasty, even though they *were* his cousins; and since they all thought that everything over there was for sale, the Crown

Council in Potsdam on the 29th debated only what price should be paid. The Chancellor was accordingly given an offer for these "tradesmen."

In warlike excitement Bethmann hurried back to Berlin: mobilisation had been decided on, but as yet suspended. Bethmann himself had written that *"mobilisation inevitably results in war."* It was late, he had asked Sir Edward Goschen to call on him at 10 P.M. on the 29th.

"Will he speak at last the word for which we have waited so long?" thought the Englishman, as he mounted the broad staircase to the Chancellor. But what words met him!

"We should like to make a bid for British neutrality."

"Suddenly," thought Goschen, "at night, without previously sounding me, and as if ready with his 'bid.'"

"Firstly, we will undertake to make no territorial acquisitions at the expense of France, should we prove victorious."

"Does that apply also to the colonies?"

"I cannot give a similar undertaking there," said Bethmann, startled; for the Potsdam offer contained no mention of this point. *"Secondly, we will respect Holland's integrity and neutrality so long as others do the same."*

"He'll be offering me the integrity of Tibet next," thought Goschen; but Bethmann went on: *"Thirdly, as regards Belgium, it will depend on the action of France what operations Germany may be forced to enter upon in Belgium. In any case, when the war is over, Belgian integrity shall be respected, if she has not sided against Germany."*

"I am dreaming," thought Goschen. "This can't possibly be the German Chancellor's room." But he forced himself to say: *"I do not think it probable that England will care to bind herself to any course of action at this stage of events. I will, however, communicate your offer to London."*

Thirty-six hours later the Englishman brought Grey's answer from London. Hearing it, Bethmann stands quite aghast, but tries to conceal his agitation: *"I am so taken up with serious matters just now that I must beg you to let me have the message as a written memorandum."*

The Englishman had thought the question of England's neutrality serious enough to make it worth while bringing the Note with him. He goes, leaving it there. England refuses, because France could well be reduced to impotence even without loss of territory: *"It would be a disgrace for us to make this bargain with Germany at the expense of France, a disgrace from which the good name of this country would never recover. The Chancellor also asks us in effect to bargain away whatever obligation or interest we have as regards the neutrality of Belgium. We could not entertain that bargain either."*

Bethmann turns the paper over and over. Was his masterpiece no masterpiece after all?

*   *

Churchill is in his element. He hawks Germany's offer all round London. Isn't it worth while making war on people like that? But all are cautious in making public decisions, for the man in the street is neither an enemy of the Serbs nor a friend of the Balkans, and the Liberal Press is still writing that the whole affair is none of our business. They had to wait for the psychological moment; everything now depended on good stage-management.

Some days before the famous Berlin offer, magnates of commerce and the Stock Exchange had come to Lloyd George and demanded neutrality, in the name of the interests which they represented. A war, even if victorious, would ruin them; neutrality would leave them eventu-

ally the bankers of Europe. When they had left,
Lloyd George began to think more kindly of the
Germans, and to support Grey again. But now,
after Bethmann's proposal?

As Grey happened to be living with Lord Haldane in Queen Anne's Gate, people were told
that diplomats were still visiting Haldane, and he
was thought to be master of the situation. In reality, not even Cambon was that, although he cross-
examined Grey twice daily and, just like the
Russian Ambassador, tried to get a definite declaration out of him. Cambon was perhaps better
informed, through the daily reports from his
brother's Embassy, of the situation in Berlin,
than Grey was from his men.

"Has the moment come at last?" asked Cambon, suppressing a sigh.

*"It will come when the position of Germany is
fully cleared up,"* said Grey uncertainly, and
went to the Cabinet meeting. Perceiving that
feeling there was wavering once more, he wired
again to Goschen: *"Gain a little respite at all
costs before any Great Power begins war!"* In
his happier moments he still hoped for the general
peace, and he tried to preserve it at all costs, for
he hated war and loved England.

"Why was I not stronger," he thought at times.

"What profit have I now of our legal liberty? We are morally bound, for all that!" What he hoped for and feared at once in those days was a split in the Cabinet.

His inner unrest grew ceaselessly. On the 30th he put his dilemma before his enemy of to-morrow, the Austrian Ambassador, with his usual frankness: *"I have been advised to take two diametrically opposite courses: either to side with Russia and France unconditionally, which might have the effect of stopping the war, or to declare that we shall remain neutral in all circumstances, which would not, however, stop the war."*

The German Ambassador attempts to learn from Grey, while simultaneously the German Kaiser asks the King what are the conditions under which they could guarantee France's neutrality. But the net is now too tightly drawn for the most willing to free himself, and Paléologue is right when he writes: *"The hour for calculations, for diplomatic tours de force is past. . . . No personal initiative, no human will could resist now the automatic mechanism of mechanical forces."* Poincaré may wire to the King that the three should unite to work together for peace; the King may answer in never so moral phrases; yet both know what this means, and the customary form

of words which both use—*"Cher et grand ami"*—
is only half true.

Yes, if Germany would demobilise, England
would force her friends to follow suit! But it is
too late for that; even if the German Kaiser were
persuaded to abdicate, next day his son would
jauntily ride in his car into the "great game" of
war.

Two more calls come faintly over the Channel
to the Kaiser's ear.

*"Belgrade is fallen, Serbia is punished, let
Austria return now. . . . Only Your Majesty can
do this. . . . God be with Your Majesty now and
always.—Daisy."*

A second private petitioner, more subtle and
more weighty, begs the Kaiser to make some proposal which he can lay before friends in Petersburg and Vienna. "Daisy" is the beautiful English Princess of Pless; the other is Lord Roths-
child.

Twenty years younger and twenty years older
respectively than the man to whom they plead,
elegant and charming, clever and powerful, they
raise their friendly voices. In vain. The Kaiser
lays "Daisy" aside; on the other message he
writes: *"An old and very much honoured acquaintance of mine!"* Attached is a note from

Zimmermann: *"Answer in the name of His Maj-esty?"* Next to it the answer: *"As cable is closed, no use.—Stumm."*

Are not these the true voices of the Wilhelm-strasse? Telegrams are going ceaselessly be-tween Berlin and London, in spite of the alleged "closing" of the cable. But there is a last, small danger that the banker with his Jewish money might interfere, as once Jacob Schiff did with the Russians in New York. Therefore: *"No use.—Stumm."*

At last the London Cabinet is relieved of this tension by means of Belgium. Churchill and Kitchener had always insisted that Germany meant to invade. Whether Belgium would de-cide to resist was doubtful: the tradition of cen-turies must make England hope for and en-courage such resistance. Had she not defended these coasts, ever since the first Edward, against Spain, the Bourbon, and Napoleon? No Great Power must be allowed to stand on that shore and look across; therefore it was invested with perpetual neutrality.

Protection of the weak! How, then, came England to refuse Bismarck's suggestion that she should guarantee Luxemburg's neutrality? That was a *demi-vierge* of sorts whose honour England

felt herself unable to guard. But the Maid of
Flanders must be no man's bride, her castle by the
sea must remain a flower-garden, unsullied by arms
or fortifications.

Gladstone had proved this once. A pioneer of
international law, a pacifist, an Englishman
through and through, Grey's predecessor and
model, he wrote in 1870 in answer to Bismarck's
revelations of Napoleon's desires: *"It would be
impossible for us to look on while liberty and independence are sacrificed."* He was sincere in his
fashion, but offered no more than was strictly necessary in support of these ideals. For at the same
time he offered both belligerent Powers Great
Britain's guarantee for Belgium; firstly, as security for international law, secondly, as security
against undue predominance of any Continental
Power—very English.

During these days all this was present to the
minds of the Cabinet, as during the succeeding
years of war it was to the British people, who
clothed their supreme interests in the mask of morality, and wisely selected the flag round which all
friends of justice were to gather. Lloyd George,
especially, wore for years this pose of the Keeper
of Justice, expounded it in brilliant speeches, and
conquered Europe's conscience, to lose it again

at Versailles. He, better than any of the rest, knew that a mere majority in the Commons was not enough to carry on this war in a country whose army was composed of volunteers, whose grown-up daughter-countries across the sea in remote continents had become independent and critical.

Besides this, he and Churchill, more than the others, were influenced by the natural wish to retain an authority which had already been shaken by the Irish question. Only war could again weaken the Conservatives; for here as everywhere Conservative circles, the lords, the squires, and the farmers, were more eager for war than the Liberal merchants and the workers, who, here as everywhere, wanted peace. Had the Liberals then been in Opposition instead of in office, they would (no one doubts it) have broken the Conservatives' will to war. As it was, however, they felt themselves strengthened by their opponents.

And yet, precisely in these last days, not only the attitude of the Cabinet, but that of Grey himself, was uncertain. His four proposals for mediation would suffice to defend him from the charge of Machiavellian cunning, even if knowledge of his character did not proclaim the contrary. But although he was a lover of peace, and though no interest of England's could cajole him into a war, he yet felt that England's honour and his own were pledged to his friends, and so in these last days he grew more and more deeply involved in the consequences of a policy of alliances which vainly protested against that name.

On the 29th he concealed from the German Ambassador, to whom he had given such grave warnings for Berlin, the fact that the Fleet was still concentrated, and consequently half mobilised. On the 30th he once more took steps to mediate in Berlin and Petersburg, and advised Paris to do the same.

But on the 31st he began to waver. This was obviously due in part to a letter and a memorandum, both urgently conceived, containing provocative arguments cleverly adapted to his character, which he received on that day from his two officials, Crowe and Nicolson. Each of these two men was a fervent champion of the Entente; Crowe, who had been thirty years at the Foreign Office, was particularly influential.

Grey had already hinted in the Cabinet that if England remained neutral he would be obliged to resign; but no one knew if Asquith might not accept his resignation, or if the counter-party, grouped round Churchill and Lloyd George, would also resign. For the split in the Cabinet

JOHN MORLEY

Member of British Cabinet, 1914–1915

threatened to grow dangerous. In the three Empires in which the ultimate decision on war or peace was the monarch's prerogative, problems of this sort did not exist, and in Paris the coalition held together; in London, however, the two wings of the ruling Liberals were at war with each other, more tacitly than openly, in the last week before August 4th; and in this struggle the prospect of the Premiership seems to have obscured, for some Ministers, the European prospect. The thought that a split of the party into two groups might leave England without a Cabinet in the moment of supreme crisis was, however, almost as bad for all English politicians as war itself. Therefore they stuck together for the time being; so late as the 31st the Cabinet repudiated any obligation and declared that neutrality was the only means of preventing a complete collapse of European credit. England's attitude could determine this *"to a very considerable degree."*

Cambon trembles with anxiety, fearing to lose France's opportunity, the fruits of the careful preparations of years. He feels like Mephistopheles when a pack of angels want to snatch Faust's soul from him, after he has worked for it so long. Yes; he has to sit quiet and let Grey tell him that Russia has precipitated the crisis, and *"would make it ap-*

pear that the German mobilisation was being forced by Russia." (An important admission against Russia.) Cambon, in reply, can only utter a warning against a repetition of England's mistake in 1870, when she "allowed an enduring increase of German strength." On August 1st, despite the declaration of war, Grey's attitude has become no firmer; nevertheless, he refuses to make Germany any promises, even if she leaves Belgium untouched. This attitude, although really too late to alter anything, would be compromising for England, had not Moltke himself admitted "that even England's neutrality itself would be too dearly bought at the price of respecting Belgium, since an offensive was only possible along the Belgian line."

In his fearful dilemma Grey now falls back on a last resort: he proposes that Germany and France shall stand under arms, facing each other on the frontier without moving; then England, as a guarantor, will remain neutral. The Germans jump at this; it looks like a miraculous chance of confining to a single front the war on two fronts which they had dreaded for decades. But when Grey transmits this reply to Cambon, he adds coldly, as though ignorant of France's obligations under her treaties: "If France cannot take advantage of this position, it is because she is bound by an alliance to which we *are not parties, and of which we do not know the terms."*

Then Cambon's excitement rises to an unprecedented pitch. He cries: *"I refuse to transmit this message to Paris! It would fill France with rage and indignation. My people would say you had betrayed us!"* Can Grey call his friend to order? Must not his heart forgive Cambon all his excitement? It is true that he has signed no blank cheque in favour of France, as Wilhelm has done for Austria; but for eight years past, and particularly during the last two years, he has repeatedly given her to understand that England will stand by her in the hour of need. And now? *"Then the German Fleet can steam into the Channel, and attack our defenceless coast!"* cries Cambon.

"That would change public opinion in England," answers Grey, retreating.

Next morning, the 2nd of August—Cambon kept all wires working and had violations of the frontier by Germany reported in the course of the session—Grey prevails on the Cabinet to guarantee the defence of the French coasts, if attacked by Germany, but only if the House of Commons consents. In that body, however, the Opposition has already declared in favour of war. The Cabinet agrees on mobilisation of the whole Fleet, which

it had refused the day before yesterday, and which
Churchill had yesterday ordered on his own responsibility. Cambon's hopes rise; feverishly he
hopes for Germany's invasion of Belgium, an act
on which all the initiated have been reckoning for
the past ten years. The more moderate Ministers
lunch together after this meeting, and it is stated
in general terms that "the Cabinet is somewhat
craftily being drawn, step by step, into war on
the side of France." After this Grey propounds
the crucial question to France and Germany,
whether they will spare Belgium. Cambon alone
gives this promise; Lichnowsky is obliged, under
orders from Berlin, to refuse a definite answer.
That was what Grey needed at this moment, although at an earlier stage he had honestly dreaded
it. At last he had a popular reason, which the man
in the street could understand, for England's participation in the war.

Four members of the Cabinet, not to speak
of Trevelyan, an excellent Under-Secretary, had
resigned on the previous day, even though the
decision for war was not yet final, having still to
be confirmed by the House of Commons. Two
of these withdrew their resignations after the violation of Belgium's neutrality. Thus there remained in the end only two men, representatives

of two worlds and two social circles: Lord Morley, seventy-six years old, the dignified President of the Privy Council, known throughout England as "Honest John," a typical English compound of literary and political ability; and John Burns, the Labour leader—who, half a century ago, as a ten-year-old boy, had been moulding and cutting candles, then made his own way wholly unassisted, became a Socialist because he found Mill too moderate, courted arrest and prison again and again; and now, after eight years in the Ministry, resigned at serious personal loss, in order to record the veto of the powerful trade unions against the war.

These were the only two men in all Europe who, being in possession of power, refused to subscribe to a decision the unrighteousness of which men in every Cabinet recognised, but preferred not to notice. With this signature which they did not give, with this power which they renounced, Morley and Burns take a more honourable place in history than all the Emperors and Princes, Generals and Ministers of State, who, during these days, thought to consolidate their power by decrees of war, and lost it in the end. For only two of the European statesmen, Lloyd George and Pashitch, who gave their signatures to the beginning of the war, re-

tained their power unbroken to its close, and both
of these lost it soon afterwards.

On the following day news came pouring in before and during the session of the House: Germany's invasion of Belgium became known at mid-
day, and King Albert's telegram appealing for
help during the session. Here the objections raised
by the minority were at first unable to make themselves heard. MacDonald, the Labour leader, confined himself in the House to a short speech against
Grey. Two days later the Labour Party voted
for the war. Feeling was divided but the opponents
of the war were in a small minority and MacDonald
at once resigned the leadership.

For the first time Grey appeared uneasy; he was
in a hurry to speak, and must have felt the historical
importance of his speech. He conquered, not because his speech was of any particular brilliance,
but because it was the only one made in Europe
in which a leader of foreign policy explained to
the representatives of a nation the reasons and
counter-reasons, interests and feelings, the whole
complex of imponderabilia, that they might decide
for themselves without restraint. In each of the
three Empires during these days war was declared
independently and without any control from two
to five times; in each case by a single man after

consultation with only a very few advisers. In France and Belgium a question was, indeed, put; but it was purely rhetorical, for of these two Parliaments the one was consulted only after the declaration of war, the other was unable to say "no." Only in England did a Minister unfold the whole picture before those responsible for the decision.

"In this present crisis, up till yesterday, we have given no promise of anything more than diplomatic support. . . . I only expressed the opinion, during the Morocco crisis, to the French Ambassador and the German Ambassador that if war was forced on France at that time, in my view public opinion in this country would have rallied to the material support of France. . . . I had authorised conversations between military and naval experts, but only on the distinct understanding that nothing which passed between them should bind either Government or restrict in any way their freedom to make a decision as to whether or not they would give their support when the time arose. . . . In 1912 it was decided that we ought to have a definite understanding in writing . . . as record that, whatever took place between military and naval experts, they were not binding engagements upon the Government." (He reads his letter to M. Cambon of November 22, 1912.) . . . *"France is involved*

*in the present crisis only because of her obligation
of honour under a definite alliance with Russia.
. . . For many years we have had a long-standing
friendship with France. . . . But how far that
friendship entails an obligation, let every man look
into his own heart, and his own feelings, and construe the extent of his obligation for himself. . . .
I speak my personal view, and I have given the
House my own feelings in the matter.*

*"The French Fleet is now in the Mediterranean,
and the Northern and Western coasts of France
are absolutely undefended. . . . If a foreign fleet
came and attacked this coast, we could not stand
aside with our arms folded. . . . I say that from the
point of view of British interests. We feel strongly
that France was entitled to know—and to know at
once!—whether or not in the event of attack upon
her unprotected Northern and Western coasts, she
could depend upon British support. . . . With
respect to Belgium, our honour and our interests
are at least as deeply involved to-day as in 1870,
and we cannot take a more narrow view or a less
serious view of our obligations than was taken by
Mr. Gladstone in 1870."* (Here he reads the replies from the two Ambassadors and King Albert's
appeal.)

"If Belgium's independence goes, the indepen-

dence of Holland will follow. I ask the House, from the point of view of British interests, to consider what will follow if we stand aside in this crisis. I doubt whether, whatever material force we may have at the end, it would be of very much value in face of the respect that we should have lost. And do not believe, whether a Great Power stands outside this war or not, it is going to be in a position at the end of it to exert its superior strength. For us, with a powerful fleet . . . if we are engaged in war, we shall suffer but little more than we shall suffer even if we stand aside; we are going to suffer, I am afraid, terribly in this war whether we are in it or whether we stand aside. Foreign trade is going to stop . . . and at the best we should not be in a position to use our force decisively to undo what had happened in the course of the war, to prevent the whole of the West of Europe opposite us falling under the domination of a single Power. . . . I believe when the country realises what is at stake, we shall be supported not only by the House of Commons, but by the determination, the resolution, the courage, and the endurance of the whole country."

In this speech everything is weighed, nothing exaggerated, little suppressed. The "sanctity of treaties" is hardly mentioned. England knew

that all Cabinets can interpret inconvenient treaties
as they like.

After this speech by the Liberal Minister, speaking against the programme of his party, in favour
of war, his Liberal friends sat moody and silent,
while the Conservatives broke into loud applause.
For Grey's words had ignored the sincere desire of
his heart, and herein lies something like a tragic
judgment on his weakness.

It was left for Asquith to tell the House of
Commons soon after, on August 6th:

*"We are fighting to vindicate the principle which,
in these days when force, material force, sometimes seems to be the dominant influence and factor
in the development of mankind, we are fighting to
vindicate the principle that small nationalities are
not to be crushed, in defiance of international good
faith, by the arbitrary will of a strong and over-
mastering Power. I do not believe that any nation
ever entered into a great controversy with a clearer
conscience; for we are fighting not for aggression,
not for the maintenance of our own selfish interests,
but in the defence of principles the maintenance of
which is vital to the civilisation of the world."*

Thus England threw into the balance her bullets
of lead, of silver—and of wind.

*   *

During these negotiations between Berlin and London there was one moment in which it seemed as though the war between France and Germany might be stopped by a guarantee from Great Britain. There was, indeed, a misunderstanding; but the treatment accorded to the case reveals in a flash the dominating nature of the army machine, which no one can stop when once he has wound it up. The horror of the Chief of the General Staff in Petersburg, when the Tsar tried to take it out of his hands, was reciprocated two days later (August 1st) by his colleague in Berlin. Thus: after that reassuring news from London, the Kaiser said to Moltke:

"Well, then, we shall simply set our whole army advancing in the East!"

Moltke: *"That is impossible, Your Majesty. The advance of an army a million strong cannot be improvised. If Your Majesty insists on sending the whole army East, you will only have a wild rabble of disorganised, armed men without supplies."*

The Kaiser: *"Your uncle would have answered me differently."*

Moltke: *"It is absolutely impossible to advance otherwise than according to plan; strong in the West, weak in the East."*

Thereupon the Kaiser wires to the King of England: *"On technical grounds my mobilisation, which had already been proclaimed this afternoon, must proceed against two fronts, East and West, as prepared. . . . I hope that France will not become nervous."* Two days later (August 1st) the Kaiser, wishing to mitigate the effect of the unavoidable threat which the advance to the frontier must convey, gives orders: *"The 16th Division in Trèves is not to proceed to Luxemburg."*

Moltke, who describes this scene, confesses: *"I felt as if my heart would break. Once again the danger arose of our advance being thrown into confusion. When I got home I was quite worn out, and I shed tears of desperation. . . . So I sat in my room, dejectedly and idle, until at 11 P.M. I was again ordered to go to His Majesty."* Explanations—mistake—war against France—advance as arranged. Moltke ends: *"I was never able to get over the impression of this event. Something in me had been destroyed, which could never be replaced; confidence and trust were shaken."*

The logic of the machine crushed its maker, and turned him into its slave. Yanushkyevitch and Moltke, in whom the thoughts, the labours, the visions, the ambitions of a lifetime had been centred on war, suffered the most terrible moments of their lives when their precious toys, set in motion at last, were suddenly bidden to stand still again. *"Something in me had been destroyed,"* writes the warrior, before beginning his own work of destruction.

CHAPTER XIII

WHAT have the masses been doing meanwhile? Have the streets of the cities emptied themselves already, sending all the men under arms to the frontier, all the women in tears to their homes? Cannot the cries of the powerless millions overwhelm ten isolated iron-bound orders from the few mighty ones? Has not Reason been at work to strengthen the victims, bidding them wrench themselves free from the sacrificial priests, deriding the sanctity of such altars?

The streets are still in uproar. Before the death-warrants blazed into the houses, the victims were still parading with threatening cries before the mysterious palaces of the pontiffs, and shouting to the silent windows their will to live.

But already they are leaderless! The chiefs of the working-people are sitting in closed rooms, even as the diplomats, sitting at tables and taking counsel hour by hour. Their chairs are harder,

314

their cigars cheaper, their coats coarser, they have no servants to shut the doors; and here you will not find the silent lackeys of diplomacy bowing obsequiously to the leather attaché-cases long after His Excellency has left. But they, too, already have their secrets from the crowd; they, too, have already become pontiffs. Already they feel in their hearts, though not yet admitting it, that to-morrow, perhaps, they must become dumb.

Perhaps. They still hope, and only the weaklings among them, only those who are wearied by long struggle, but have toiled and saved a secure position for their children, now go over to the idea of nationalism and long to agree, for once, with the Government.

Berlin: *"The meeting announced for Sunday in the Treptower Park is directed against the war. For that reason it may be feared that to hold it in the present serious situation might prove dangerous to the public security."* Woe to him who raises his voice against war! Why, he might preserve the peace! In thirty-nine popular meetings the Socialists try to attain under a roof that which was forbidden under the open sky. In vain. Two days later they try it once again in seventeen meetings. The Police disperse them all.

It feels itself to be strong. It reads the *Vor-*

wärts and hears how, muttering sullenly, it wavers: *"We will not live through the coming events with fatalistic indifference.. We shall remain true to our cause, convinced of the lofty greatness of our mission of civilisation. The first enactments of martial law strike the workers' movement with fearful severity. Rashness, and useless and ill-judged sacrifices at this moment, damage not only the individual but also our cause. We call upon you to be patient until, despite all, the future belongs to Socialism, the bond between peoples."*

The Social Democrat, Hofmann, in the Bavarian Landtag: *"We are standing on the brink of an historical event which may endanger the existence of the German Empire, and will perhaps mean calling upon the last man to defend his fatherland. If, in a few days, the German people should be called to arms, the Social Democrats, too, will defend their fatherland."*

When the party began this retreat, it felt: "Four million electors are too weak for a revolution; therefore we must submit. We will obey, but under protest; never will we vote the money in the Reichstag for the great murder. Our sullen silence shall show our brothers, the enemy, yonder, what we are feeling. We shall soon shake hands over the officers' heads."

This appears to have been the decision taken by most of them; few speak differently during the first deliberations. No resolution is passed. A representative is sent hurriedly to Paris to take counsel with Jaurès, who promised the German Haase faithfully, the day before yesterday, to resist. The best thing would be to pronounce a veto in identical terms in the Parliaments of all centres of war. On the same evening Herman Müller travels to Paris, carrying Germany's conscience to the enemy.

Yet the German workers are Germans. They have, indeed, been reviled for thirty years past as a rabble without a fatherland, and yet they like to remember their two years of military service. Now another occasion offers to leave the treadmill, and the State will look after the children at home. Danger? As though the boiler might not burst to-morrow!—besides, not every bullet finds a billet. The leaders, however, who know that the crowd outside is thinking that it is too weak to revolt, find one slogan to soothe their consciences: The bloodthirsty Tsar is our enemy!

Bethmann acts diplomatically. Quick, now, to publish the Kaiser's peace telegrams, but suppress all our efforts of the past four weeks to drive one another into war; and, finally, suppress the Tsar's suggestion of The Hague! Up! Remember your Bebel, who wanted to fight against the Tsar. We are fighting for liberty against the barbarian's government by the knout!

If but three points of the foreign negotiations had been brought out so cleverly as was this one point of internal policy, the world-war would have been avoided. In the one case arrogance begat frivolity, in the other fear begat caution. If it proved possible, in this war of illogical alliances, to spread a general illusion of a holy war against Asiatic hordes, the Red Flag would have to be rolled up; possibly even its battle front might be split.

Already the voices are out of accord.

The *Badische Volkfreund: "In this fearfully grave hour party passions must be dumb. . . . Social Democracy has done all that was in its power to avert war. It repudiates all responsibility for things having gone so far as they have. Its policy has been directed, not since yesterday or the day before, but for decades past, towards averting such a fearful catastrophe."*

The *Chemnitzer Volksstimme: "But one question obsesses us all: shall we be victorious? . . . Foremost in our consciousness is our duty of fighting against the tyranny of the Russian knout.*

*Germany's women and children shall not fall vic-
tims to Russian bestiality. For if the Triple Entente conquers, it will not be an English Governor
or a French Republican who will rule over Germany, but the Tsar of Russia. . . . Not with thoughtless shouting and not with hate against the Russian workmen, not with God for the King, but for
German liberty, our comrades will take the field,
resolved to let no arm-chair patriots surpass them
in the fulfilment of their duty towards the fatherland."*

The *Essener Arbeiterzeitung: "If this country
is threatened to-day by Russia's decisions, then,
inasmuch as the struggle is one against the blood-
thirsty Russian Tsarism, the perpetrator of a million crimes against liberty and civilisation, Social-
Democrats will let none in the land surpass them
in devotion to duty and sacrifice. . . . Down with
Tsarism! Down with the last refuge of barbarism!
That shall be our watchword!"*

Up, German miner! Thy brother from the
neighbouring pit in Lorraine, whose shaft comes so
near thine own that thou canst almost hear his
hammer knock, him shalt thou shoot down at the
pleasure of the German God and the order of the
King; yet think, as thou takest aim, think with all
the passion of thy soul that thou lovest thy brother,

who falls beneath thy hand; and hatest the King
to whom thou hast sworn that all this on the Marne
is being done only because the bloodstained Tsar
would else rule over Germany, and abandon thy
daughters to shame!

The confusion exists, but it is not yet universal.
On the same day the *Leipziger Volkszeitung* describes its brothers as "dubious tyrannicides" and
issues a warning against quoting Marx and Bebel,
who supported the Russian war of old, in the
present crisis, since *"to-day the sons of those who
stood on the barricades are supporting the altars
and crowns which their fathers and grandfathers
made to totter. . . . Who shall maintain that a Central European State which wages war against
Russia is carrying the revolution into Russia to-
day! . . . The plan of the German Government is
to goad the German workmen into war with Russia
by appealing to an outworn ideology. The swindle
is patent."*

Even after the declaration of war the *Vorwärts*
waxes sarcastic over the attempt to represent this
war as wanted by the Socialists, and warns their
leaders not to countenance it by voting with the
majority in the Reichstag; for then the Tsar would
exclaim, "That is the news I was waiting to hear!
Now the backbone of our own revolution is broken!

Now I can loose the dogs of nationalism. I am saved!"

To-morrow the *Vorwärts* will have to take another tone, for to-day the die is cast. Only two days ago the Party Headquarters told the Chancellor that they would be obliged to vote against the war credits. What of to-day?

They sit now in their Committee-room, a hundred strong. Side by side with furrowed faces of the people, artisans, whose fists crash on the table when their rough voices are raised in excitement; side by side with reckless-looking desperadoes who wear only stiff beards, over-wide collars, old patched neckties, sit teachers and lawyers, in outward appearance similar to the middle classes from which they spring. The representatives of the Majority rise among them and say:

"The new White Book issued by the Government shows that Russia first mobilised, then refused to wait for our declaration of war and crossed the frontier. In the West, too, it is officially reported that the French are already on German soil; the war is therefore one of defence! In such a case we ought not to vote against war credits, almost half of which are for the benefit of the widows and children of the poor. As we are only a quarter of the House and at best could not prevent the credits from being passed, our refusal would only awaken an impression amongst the masses that we are indifferent to, or perhaps even welcome invasion and defeat. Only those who are strong enough to seize the reins of government dare proclaim a general strike. In other circumstances civil war helps only the enemy." So speak the Majority.

Kautsky, the best brain in the room, is for abstaining from voting, as Bebel had done in 1870. He is, however, unsupported.

For the Minority, under Haase, Lebedour, and Liebknecht, repudiates any comparison with those old days when only two Socialists sat in the Reichstag. "To-day there are one hundred and ten of them, representing nearly one-third of the people. The White Books may be deceptive! Why should the Government, which we have always mistrusted, be assumed to be speaking the truth to-day? As we are the strongest party in Europe, our consent would have a deplorable effect everywhere, and would probably destroy the International. Telegrams forwarded yesterday and to-day from London, Paris, Milan, and Brussels, urge us to resist. He who votes the money must share the responsibility for the conduct and aims of the war. The Chancellor must be required to bind himself this very day to make no annexations; he will refuse to do so, and then our refusal of the money will open the eyes of the masses."

The struggle goes on for hours. The Minority considers giving a separate vote, but rejects the plan in order not to weaken the party. Those who would serve God and those who would serve Mammon still try to find a unifying dogma. A vote is taken. 78 to 14. Haase, the President, submits to discipline and undertakes to read out in the Reichstag a Statement of Policy with which he disagrees. The Minority had secured only the adoption of one single sentence. *"As soon as the war becomes a war for annexations we shall direct our sharpest efforts against it."* The last cry of the pacifist conscience! When this declaration was laid before the Chancellor that evening, he asked that this all-important reservation should be deleted in that form. The interview was a private one. The sentence, in that form, *was* deleted.

The attitude of the German Socialists caused such surprise abroad that the Bucharest Socialist paper, a week later, was still maintaining the report to be a lie, and sneering at the inflexible *Arbeiterzeitung* of Vienna (whose Berlin reports it had before it) as a new Governmental organ.

As the Austrian party had only one million electors and was much weaker than the German, Vienna had been obliged to come even sooner into line. The Government could venture to write in its paper: *"According to reliable information there are in the Austro-Hungarian Monarchy a large number of subversive elements which endanger the security of the public and of the State in the highest degree. The Government therefore appeals to the national patriotism to make these dangerous elements harmless in every respect. . . . Information in the above sense can be handed in at the War Supervisory Office in the Ministry of War."*

For two weeks Austria's Socialists had fought passionately against Berchtold's provocations. To-day they heard *"the iron voices of history, the veil is torn away from the impudent intrigues of Tsar-ist policy!"* What the leaders really felt, however, flashed out from the ironical sentence at the close: *"'Life for the Tsar'—this sanguinary world-farce is being played by the whole of civilised humanity in melodramatic style!"* Nevertheless, the day when Berlin agreed to the money was celebrated in the *Arbeiterzeitung* of Vienna as *"a day of the proud-est and loftiest exaltation of the German spirit."* And thus it was in Budapest and Prague, in Lem-berg and Klagenfurt, among all the peoples of Austria.

The reason? Betrayal of the peoples by the Governments of Europe!

In the case of three of the five great Cabinets this can be proved by documentary evidence.

In England tradition forbids such betrayal, and the control of the Ministers by the House of Commons makes it impossible. The British documents —the only series issued by a Government of its own free will, for in the three Empires the publication was due to the Revolution—have stuck to this old English principle. Nearly all attempts to construe differences of form between the Blue Book of August 1914 and the collected Documents of 1926 into falsifications have broken down; there are differences, but none of any importance. Naturally, there are gaps, but very little has been left out for England's special benefit. It is, however, true that Grey's loose obligations to France and Russia in 1912 and 1914 were undertaken without the knowledge of the House of Commons, and even kept secret by him from half the Cabinet, so that the *Manchester Guardian* was able to write on August 4th: *"Sir Edward Grey's speech last night showed that for years he has been keeping back the whole truth."* In the decisive days a certain portion of the Press also conspired to stir the peaceful people to madness with criminal

lies about German invasions, excesses, and intentions.

The French Yellow Book cannot yet be checked;
but here, too, falsifications can be deduced indirectly; the very fact that four months were
needed to bring it out is suspicious. French friends
of the truth have already pointed out five falsifications. These show that the knowledge possessed by
the French Government of Russia's general mobilisation was concealed from the people, France's own
desire for peace exaggerated, Germany shown as
wanting war. Two of these documents are well-
nigh pure inventions; Poincaré, in reply to later
questions, made a lame attempt to explain this as
*"dictated by consideration for the secrecy of the
cipher."* Further ground for doubting the genuine nature of this Yellow Book is to be found in
the opinion of the French jurist Larnaude, Dean
of the Faculty of Law in Paris, and of Monsieur
Lapradelle, Professor of International Law, who,
working for an official commission during the
peace negotiations, based the *"criminal responsibility of William II,"* among other grounds, on
the so-called *"Hun letter"* of the Kaiser, in which
he was alleged to have written to Franz Joseph:
*"My heart bleeds, but all must be devastated with
fire and sword; neither tree nor house must be*

*left standing. With these deeds of terror, which
alone are able to crush so degenerate a people as
the French, the war will be ended within two
months; while if I allowed considerations of humanity to prevail, it might drag out for years."*
The free inventions in this letter are the more astonishing when one considers that its authors
expected a nation renowned for its psychological
sense to believe in a document imagined with so
little psychological subtlety. The famous *"official
and secret memorandum on the reinforcement of
the German Army"* in the Yellow Book of April
13th, alleged to be Ludendorff's work, was also an
obvious invention.

The falsifications of the Russian Government
were exposed by the publications of the Bolsheviks:
seventy-nine documents were published on August
7, 1914; to-day two hundred and eight are known.
Of the documents published at the outbreak of
war, about a quarter are falsified, particularly the
telegrams between Sazonov in Petersburg and his
Ambassador in Paris, Isvolski. The intention
was to make Germany appear unconditionally desirous of war, whereas she really urged localisation
of the conflict, and her desire for war was thus
only conditional; further, to suppress everything
that could be interpreted as a real desire for war

on the part of France and Russia. The reports of Russia's own preparations for war were minimised; those of Austria exaggerated.

The worst liar was Count Berchtold. He took six months before issuing sixty-nine documents in his Red Book to the subjects of Austria. Four years later the Revolution published three hundred and eighty-two as *"Appendix and Supplement"*; these include the most important sources for the question of war guilt. Of Berchtold's sixty-nine documents nine cannot be checked, twelve could not be falsified because they were known to other Powers, ten have been reproduced correctly. Thirty-eight—that is, more than half of the fifty-seven susceptible of falsification—have in fact been falsified.

Among these falsifications we may particularise the following:

In Number Six the Minister at Belgrade wrote that *"the moment is a favourable one (for war), and both the foreign and internal political situations offer favourable prospects and opportunities —probably the last that our age will see."* In the Red Book this undisguisedly provocative sentence is omitted altogether. The Ultimatum and commentary are ante-dated by two days (comp. Berlin). Monsieur Bienvenu's remarks have been reproduced where favourable to Austria (Number Eleven), but the important addition, *"The Minister of Justice has, of course, no influence on the conduct of foreign policy,"* is omitted.

In Number Thirteen the warning issued by the Paris Cabinet before Russia's Ultimatum is omitted. The report of Serbia's mobilisation is combined with the report of the rupture of relations out of several telegrams (Numbers Twenty-three and Twenty-four) in such a way as to make it appear that the mobilisation in Serbia had influenced the rupture of relations by Austria, while the reverse was actually the case.

In Number Twenty-eight, a telegram from Petersburg dated July 26, the all-important ending has been left out. This had contained the following testimony from the German Military Attaché: *"Had the impression of great nervousness and anxiety. Believe wish for peace to be genuine. . . . Undercurrent of feeling: hope in Germany for mediation by His Majesty."*

Many peaceful proposals by Sazonov, *e.g.* that of July 27th, that the King of Italy (in other words, an ally of the enemy) should mediate, are omitted in Number Thirty-one.

Berchtold authorised his Ambassador in Berlin to make a declaration that he *"intends no annexa-*

tion" (Number Thirty-two); but the all-important addition that he is *"not to enter on a binding engagement"* is omitted.

In Number Thirty-eight two passages proving Sir Edward Grey's peaceable views are omitted.

In a telegram to Berlin (Number Forty-two) General Conrad von Hötzendorff, whose name makes a sudden appearance in the original, is banished from the revised version; the fact being that on the 28th, and therefore before the Russian mobilisation, he had demanded *"that both Austria-Hungary and (in view of the whole situation) Germany also, should take immediate and far-reaching counter-measures."* The incriminating telegram from Count Szögyény of July 28th is omitted altogether, because it shows Berlin as rejecting England's mediation and passing the proposal on to Vienna only as a matter of form. Berchtold's answer in his Red Book is the exact opposite of what documents later discovered have proved to be the case.

Then Bethmann's warning of the 28th, containing the intimation of England's threat (Number Forty-four), is falsified. Number Forty-seven contains eight falsifications. This is a telegram from the Austrian Ambassador in Petersburg. In it the decisive effect on Sazonov of the bombard-

ment of Belgrade is suppressed altogether, together with the statement that the Russian mobilisation (which was taken on the strength of that
act) has no aggressive purpose.

Number Fifty-six omits Sazonov's declarations
that the mobilisation does not as yet mean war,
and that he was relieved by the conversation—
which seemed to him to be meant seriously.

On August 3rd the German Government submitted to the Reichstag a dossier consisting of
thirty numbers and seven supplementary documents; when the "real German documents" were
issued by the Revolution in 1919 they had increased to the number of over seven hundred. If
we leave out the seven supplementary numbers
and confine ourselves to those among the thirty
over which there can be no dispute, seven of these
must be set aside at once as not susceptible of falsification, since they were known to the enemy. Of
the twenty-three documents susceptible of falsification, the Government falsified eighteen. A whole
series of these relates to the points on which Germany must admit part responsibility for the war;
the intention to conceal these from the people is
thus patent. From among these falsifications we
select the following:

Exhibit One, comprising the circular against

Serbia, is post-dated from the 21st to the 23rd of July to conceal the fact that the German Government identified itself with it even after learning the text of Vienna's Ultimatum, which it pretended that it had not seen before the enemy did.

In Exhibit Eighteen, a telegram from the Prussian General in Petersburg, dated July 30th, the decisive sentence is omitted: *"I have the impression that they have mobilised here from a dread of coming events without any aggressive intentions, and are now frightened of what they have brought about."*

In Exhibit Eleven the final sentence by the German Military Attaché in Petersburg: *"Believe wish for peace to be genuine,"* is omitted.

In Exhibit Twenty-four, the German Ultimatum to Russia, the important sentence at the conclusion, which showed Russia's belief that Germany had already mobilised, is omitted.

In Exhibit Twenty-seven, Viviani's answer to the Ultimatum, his hope that Great Britain would mediate and that the two principal belligerents would listen to reason is omitted, in order to give the impression of a brusque refusal and of the inevitability of the German declaration of war.

Above all, all incriminating documents sent to and from Vienna are omitted. With a laudable

skill which the German diplomats displayed only
after the expiration of the decisive month of July,
only, in fact, on August 1st, and solely for the purpose of misleading their own people, all mistakes
of their own Government and nearly all warnings
from foreign Governments have been omitted. The
German reader or editor was not to learn anything
of Berchtold's crime, of Bethmann's weakness, of
Wilhelm's blank cheque, of Grey's further attempts
at mediation; the Kaiser's subjects were shown
only the Tsar's perfidy, Sir Edward's guile, Viviani's refusal. Thus the man in the street, even the
Liberal or Social Democrat Deputy, could only
say: "Yes, we have been brutally attacked! Up
and defend our Fatherland against aggression!"
Had the Imperial German Government published
only a portion of the decisive documents on August 3rd, the German Socialists would on the 4th
have voted to a man against the war credits. In
justified anticipation of this fact, the Government
falsified the White Book.

* *

In Russia, the other power besides Austria
guilty of aggression, the resistance of the workers
had risen to a pitch shortly before the crisis, as
though in a kind of presentiment; for it had been

smouldering for decades past. One hundred and
fifty thousand men are said to have gone on strike.
By the middle of July the price of foodstuffs had
risen threefold in and around the two chief cities.
Communication by tram and ship had broken
down, the small-arms factories were shut, the railways idle, the telegraph-wires pulled down. Even
the Minister of the Interior, surrounded as he was
by war-mongers, said as late as July 28th: *"The
war can never become popular in the deepest heart
of our masses."*

But no party was allowed to speak or to print
its views. So the mobilisation finds the workers
sullen and silent; dumbly they stand on that morning before the little red posters, hanging low but
conspicuous, like the handbills for the strike: the
Imperial orders to the Army. Then a man comes
along, sticks the cockade in their caps; now they
are marked men. The rest proceeds automatically,
or by force. In the factories they warn one another softly not to murmur. Their instinct tells
them in advance that war will lead to revolution.

Thousands of others cried their protest to
Heaven. In Vilna recruits threw themselves on
the ground, refusing to enter the cattle-trucks. In
Charkov for a whole day they dared not put the
strikers in uniform; in Abo recruits, as soon as

they got their uniforms, hurried to sell their foot-gear and underclothes and fled as they were, so that military boots could be bought for thirty co-pecks.

But there is one place of assembly in Russia which is not closed, and at its door the Cossacks do not hew down the workman who draws near; stand-ing erect they honour his arrival. There in the Duma, before the Ionic columns, where the Court, the nobility, and society in all its glory come thronging to-day to fill the draughty Imperial boxes, loyal and warlike speeches are, indeed, made; but after them a grey-headed man, with a glance of steel, demands liberty to speak. *"We may not speak as we would, as men in other coun-tries do. The Government grants the people no amnesty, only heavy taxes. Steel your spirit, workers and peasants; gather your forces, and when you have defended your country, liberate it!"*

It is Kerensky who so speaks. He, too, votes for the credits. He, too, believes in Russia's purely defensive good conscience, or forces himself to be-lieve in it. None the less, it is open incitement to Revolution! Three years from to-day he will be ruling here; while they who scowled at him be-tween the Ionic columns will be biting their lips in *"holes and corners or in foreign lands."* But more violent still is the next speaker, Shustov, who speaks at once for the Socialists and for the five Bolsheviks. He refuses the war credits. *"Our hearts beat in unison with those of our brothers in Europe. We cannot prevent this war of emperors, but we will end it. This is the last act of barbarism. We peoples will conclude peace, not you diplomats!"* We are in Russia—and does this dark, quivering man not fear to leave his life behind when he leaves the platform or the hall? Who prevents the Grand Duke outside from cutting him down? Does one single voice like his ring out from the forum of the freer lands?

In spite of that, a few days later the President of the Duma lies to the French Ambassador: *"The war has suddenly put an end to all our internal controversies. All parties in the Duma have only one thought, to fight against Germany. The Russian people has experienced no such wave of patriotic emotion since 1812."*

* * *

In England, where the Liberal Government itself slid rather than walked into war, the Socialists had an easier task; and here, soon five sects were to stand in varying degrees of opposition to the war. This Party has the credit of having composed the best manifesto in Europe: not a "clarion call," but truths; not sentimentality, but sense; a masterpiece!

DOWN WITH THE WAR.

Workers of Great Britain, you have no quarrel with the workers of Europe. They have no quarrel with you. The quarrel is between the RULING classes of Europe.

DON'T MAKE THEIR QUARREL YOURS.

One million Trade Unionists and Socialists of Germany have protested against the war.

DON'T DESERT THEM.

Workers of Great Britain, unite with the organised workers of France and Russia in saying that though our Governments declare war, we declare peace.
Stand true in this hour of crisis. The flag of International Solidarity is greater than the flag of Britain, of Germany, of France, of Austria, of Russia. It waves over all.
Why should you go to war? What have you to gain from war? What has war ever done

for you? What did the last war—the Boer War—do for you? Twenty thousand workers were shot dead on the battle-field. You are still paying £12,000,000 every year in food-taxes for it. The workers of South Africa are worse off than ever. The rich mine-owners alone benefited.

THE WORKERS NEVER BENEFIT BY WAR . . .

This is a war of the RULING Classes. But the RULING Classes will not fight. They will call on you to fight. . . .
Workers, even now you can stop this terrible calamity if you will! No Government can continue to engage in war if its people say with sufficient strength: THERE MUST BE PEACE.

SAY IT!

Say it in your thousands. March through the streets and say it. Gather together in your squares and market-places and say it. Say it everywhere. . . .

DOWN WITH THE WAR!

They said it everywhere; in their tens of thousands they flocked together on Sunday afternoon and clamoured, for here no one forbade the man

in the street to say what he felt; no one prevented
the crowd from listening to him. In all Europe
it was only in England that during these days no
meeting, speech, or newspaper was proscribed. It
rained. The Column was lost in mist. Nelson, on
its top, was no more than a spectre. It was just
that spectre of the War-Hero which they intended
to exorcise. Old Keir Hardie stood on the steps
and spoke. The crowd nodded and shouted, but
were orderly, like Englishmen.

Then up Pall Mall come a few hundred young
fellows, some of them Frenchmen—one can hear
it in their shouts; the national flags flap together
in the rain; now there are some six hundred of
them. Some of them wish to speak. The workers
interrupt them. They drag them down from the
steps. While they are applauding Henderson's
resolution against the war, the war-demonstrators
are shouting in front of the German Embassy: *"A
bas les Prussiens!"* Then they march up to Buck-
ingham Palace, where the King does not show himself at the window, for now they are growling the
Marseillaise.

A week later all is transformed. The majority
of the Socialists are now in favour of recruiting the
volunteers, soon even the Fabians join in, and the
most radical of all, the Independent Socialists, no

longer hold their men back from supporting the war against war. Only a few remain incorruptible. MacDonald writes with noble courage:

"We are not fighting for the independence of Belgium. We are fighting because we are in the Triple Entente; because the policy of the Foreign Office for a number of years has been anti-German, and because that policy has been conducted by secret diplomacy on lines of creating alliances in order to preserve the balance of power."

The reason of this great change was the invasion of Belgium; now they felt themselves once again to be the Police of Europe.

*   *

Brussels had to give in.

The streets still echoed with the march of tens of thousands, the circus arena still reeked with dust, with the shouts and pantings of the heated crowd, in whose midst Jaurès had conjured the name of peace. By Saturday the *Comité Fédéral* was calling men and women to join in a monster demonstration on the following Monday.

But on Sunday all was cancelled. In the three days, July 30th to August 1st, Belgium's destiny had darkened with fearful rapidity. Vandervelde, who but yesterday had dominated the crowd in the

RT. HON. RAMSAY MACDONALD
Leader of the Labour Party, 1914–

circus, now kept going in and out of the Ministry. In its rooms he pledged his great party to stand with the nation if the threatened invasion of the Germans became a reality, and even consented himself to enter the Government; and in the People's House, at a session of the Party Committee, he drew up the manifesto for the morrow:

"We Socialists are not responsible. To-day the catastrophe has come, and the fatal force of events has filled us with one sole thought; soon we may have to defend our country against invasion. Then we shall fight with double fire because we shall be defending the existence of our country against militarist barbarism. . . . But even in the blackest hour forget not that we belong to the International; remain fraternal and kind, so far as such an attitude can be reconciled with the defence of our native soil."

The next day the Party organ actually called on its readers to volunteer for service: *"for it is better to die for the idea of humanity than to bow down to the law of the Huns and Vandals."*

* *

The decision of the masses lay in Paris.

Germany's party was the largest, but it still stood, now as forty years previously, in absolute opposition to the Government; and to proclaim the General Strike was merely to choose between international and civil war. France had already seen many Socialist Governments, and Viviani, the Premier, and Malvy, the young Minister of the Interior, had been Socialist not so long ago, if they had turned somewhat bourgeois since. It is true that they and the men of the *Humanité* attacked one another with all the bitterness of widely opposed sects, but their spheres touched, and personally they were not inimical. Society, the Army, and the Nobility were full of radical leaders, were saturated with their literature; their cultures met and blended; here none was legitimate and none was outcast. The salutary consequence was that during these days the opposing leaders in Paris remained in close mutual contact; and since it is in the great cities that the gulf between the classes is widest (because they live in such close proximity), it was only between the extreme wings that understanding was impossible; between Clemenceau and Renaudel, between *revanche* and friendship.

The heads of the State were still far from Paris; at last Poincaré saw the coast of France and leapt into his special train at Dunkirk, to hurry to Paris. When he arrived at noon on

Thursday he was welcomed at the station like a
victorious Marshal by Officers, Admirals, Deputies, Academicians, Poets. But amid all the tumult the President's eyes remained glued to those
of Isvolski and of the British Ambassador, who
shook his hand in silence. Outside the crowd
pressed round the Gare du Nord; there were
flowers, flags, shouts, songs; and from his carriage
an Admiral shouted these pregnant words to the
intoxicated mob: *"Be silent! There are hours in
which silence means all. It is not for us to command Providence, but my heart tells me that when
the hour strikes, France will be ready!"*

Next day Jaurès, with a hundred others, arrived at the same station amid similar scenes of
excitement, not coming from the Tsar, only from
the peoples who had sworn brotherhood; impa-
tient as the President to reach Paris. Both leaders took counsel with their friends and their foes.
Jaurès, still full of the fervour of the Brussels
crowd, still thrilled by the oath sworn by his German comrades, had written only yesterday in a
manifesto: *"The Socialist Party proclaims aloud
that only France can dispose of France's fate;
that in no circumstances must she be involved,
through the more or less arbitrary exploitation of
secret treaties and unknown obligations, in a*

*frightful conflict, and that she must keep her full
liberty of action, to be able to exert an influence
in favour of peace over Europe . . . Should Russia, however, not yield to it, it is our duty to declare that we know only one treaty: the treaty
which binds us to the human race."* To-day he is
anxious; what is going to happen? Here, it
seems, even the most loyal comrades are talking
of the possibility of attack by Germany.

On the evening of the 30th, at six monster
meetings in Paris and at many others in pro-
vincial towns they give the masses their slogan:
General Strike and Peace! But it was in chas-
tened mood that Jaurès wrote his article for the
next morning. That which had appeared this
morning had been written in Brussels, and seemed
still imbued with full confidence.

This evening, between fresh threatening telegrams from Berlin and the suppressed agitation
of Paris, he writes for the first time of an attack
by Germany, though he does describe it as im-
probable. To-day the danger does not lie in the
Cabinets, but *"in the universal nervousness, and
sudden impulses born of fear. . . . Therefore,
calm, reason! All are invited to the Salle Wa-
gram on Sunday, where resolutions will be passed.
Unremitting action, vigilance of the spirit: those*

are the true sentry-posts of Reason!" A soul
overshadowed, fearful of succumbing to compulsion; only yesterday it spat scorn on the criminals
everywhere, to-day it recommends to others the
calm which it has to compel itself to feel; it post-
pones final decisions, and preserves a statesmanlike silence on the problems not yet besetting the
crowd.

For next day, when the article appears, Jaurès
is negotiating with the Government on behalf of
his followers about the possibility of saving peace.
The interview, the course of which is not definitely known even to-day, seems to have paved the
way towards an understanding.

Why?

Like his German comrades, he feels that even
the worker wishes to protect himself and his loved
ones against assault. But above all, Jaurès wants
to be at hand, to keep close watch on the Ministers,
to catch them out in the lies they are already pre-
paring in the guise of frontier violations, and by
gaining the confidence of the Government, to whom
his support is of inestimable value, to be able to
cry to them in the crucial moment: "You lie! The
Germans are not stirring a foot. You would only
take half the German force from off the shoulders
of the accursed Tsar, and provoke them to anger

for the sake of Alsace!" I must try, he thinks, to
teach our German comrades by common sense,
threats, and craft, that to which an old-fashioned
Constitution forbids them direct access; then perhaps after all we shall manage to avert what seems
inevitable!

Cool blood and reason! He feels that to-day is
the decisive day of his life. He hurries back from
the war-sick Ministry into the pacific offices of the
Humanité. *"What shall we tell the masses to-
morrow morning? How explain it?"* Then the
telephone brings a voice from Brussels. A German comrade is on his way to Paris. Excitement,
fresh hopes!

Late in the evening they leave the offices to dine.
They do not see the young man waiting at the
street entrance; but he sees them and follows. Rue
Montmartre, Café du Croissant. They sit down
at the regular table, with the old sofa set between
the windows. It is hot, and the windows are open;
the night is breathless, the little curtains hang
limply down. Jaurès is excited, hopeful of the
German's mission to-morrow.

Then a hand comes through the open window
and pushes the curtain aside. No one has time to
see it. Two shots ring out. Everyone leaps to
his feet; but Jaurès has collapsed on the sofa by

the window. They lay his great form across two marble-topped tables; he makes a pitifully helpless movement with his hand, a red stream gushes from his head, and for a minute Jean Jaurès' brain is seen beating before the eyes of all. He is unconscious; they bind napkins round his head. Doctors shake their heads. Fifteen minutes later he is dead. When a carriage brought home the pale, bleeding corpse thousands were already thronging the street. Pater Patriæ, they felt in their dumb hearts. Many wept. At midnight the news was ringing through all the streets of Paris.

Villain, the murderer, narrowly saved from lynching, a young, pale, and calm student, with no trace of fanaticism in features or manner, words or attitude, looking like a clerk, son of a town recorder, says in the dock: *"I made up my mind to kill the opponent of the three years' Military Service. He was too harmful to France; I meant to shoot at the door of his office, but was unable."* Perhaps he could not endure the calm glance of that great man? A curtain gave him courage, by screening from him the enemy of his fatherland.

"Fellow-citizens! A fearful murder has been committed. Jaurès, the great speaker who used to adorn the forum of France, has been murdered in dastardly fashion. I bare my head at the grave

*of this Socialist who fought for such great things,
and who in these difficult days supported the patriotic attitude of the Government in its pursuit
of peace!"* This proclamation stands next morning in large letters on every street corner of Paris.
Is it an appeal by the party? It is the Government itself, headed by Viviani. They surely remember that only a few days ago the dead man
found these words for his Fatherland: *"The nation
is a treasure-house of human genius and progress,
and it would ill befit the proletariat to destroy this
precious vessel of human culture."*

Poincaré, probably much relieved at the lucky
course taken by this bullet, writes a feeling letter
to the widow. The hostile Press writes: *"A political criminal of great gifts. He almost invariably
spoke against France. But just now, at this crisis,
he seemed to be changing his attitude."*

Was it a false dawn? He fell on the last evening of July; one night parted him from that 1st
of August which decided the fate of Europe; half
a day more from the arrival of the German. Perhaps all depended on that coming conversation,
in which two minorities of similar views had hoped
to strengthen one another and become a majority.
Then or never all depended on the force and genius
of a personality capable of inspiring his terrified

friends with courage, his brave enemies with terror; on a man like this, whose death even the
Government which hated him mourned, like An-
tony, in the forum of Paris.

This murder was committed five weeks after
the Serb had shot the Hapsburg. Two young
nationalists, acting on conviction, shot the leaders
whom they held to be the enemies of their Father-
lands. But their thoughts and illusions were as
different as their names; Princip and Villain, the
conscientious and the evil. Princeps and Villanus:
Prince and Serf. To strike the secular fetters
from the limbs of millions of oppressed Slavs: that
was a great aim. To renew the war with Germany
for the sake of Alsace and Lorraine, a country of
mixed population and uncertain sympathies, seems
a more questionable one. To set forty million men
fighting on the one side and sixty million on the
other in order that at the end a dubious residue of
a million and a half should move from one side
to the other—that "comes in very questionable
shape."

The first shot unleashed destiny, the second removed the last obstacle; but Princip has become a
national hero, while his victim is forgotten. Villain is forgotten, but the living force of his victim emerges more and more distinctly, and from

his example millions of every tongue have formed for themselves a symbol of liberty.

The next day, while Germany was declaring war in Petersburg; while four countries were marching against each other in a life-and-death struggle, the comrades of Jaurès and a Belgian are sitting with the German in the Palais Bourbon, whose corridors are seething with hatred of Germany; six friends from the lower classes, citizens of three enemy countries, consider how to call a halt to the armies of Emperors and Presidents as they advance in their millions. Capable and well-meaning, but overwhelmed and already quite hopeless; hence no spark leaps from their souls. They bow before the force of circumstances which they should be moulding, abandon the general strike, negotiate only about the credits. What is the reason? The lies of their Governments, which they could not but believe.

The German says positively that in Berlin they talk only of rejection or abstention. The French declare that if Germany attacks, no Frenchman could refuse the money for his nation's defence. The idea of issuing an identical manifesto to abstain from voting in both Berlin and Paris breaks down, *"principally because telegraphic communication has ceased."*

After this correct but tragi-comic statement, the German leaves Paris, both parties retaining full liberty of action.

The leaders proceed to defend their patriotic attitude in monster meetings, pointing out the devoted efforts of their Government in favour of peace. With their forefathers of 1793 they cry as Revolutionaries, "Peace to the huts, war to the palaces!" But they end their speeches as Frenchmen: *"For the Fatherland! For the Republic!"* To a man they will rush to arms to defend France against Germany; their feelings are precisely those of their German brothers, who imagine that they are defending themselves against Russia. No; these are no traitors—they are, all of them, merely betrayed. For just as a Russian peasant had no feeling against Germany, so no German burgher or workman could have any feeling against France. In both countries alike a handful of men seduced the nation into the mad illusion that westward there was something to hate, something to conquer.

*   *

It was a Roumanian who hit off the position of the masses in these days in a few brilliant words. The Serbs, the Belgians, and the French, he wrote, are acting in justified self-defence; they are bound to defend their countries; but the others have nothing left to do, once war has been declared, but *"with curses against war on their lips and with the oath to fight against it after peace is declared, to take the field, and with bleeding heart turn soldiers. The Governments still have the power to impose on us the tragic necessity of setting brother to shoot at brother."*

CHAPTER XIV

THE AVALANCHE

EUROPE is burning. Nevertheless, not one pure flame goes up from any Cabinet; not even in the ultimate hours did they commit themselves openly to the game of fear and hatred to which they had incited their peoples. Jagow was no sentimentalist; putting all lies aside, he said to Goschen, the British Ambassador, who had asked for his passports on August 4th, after Germany's last refusal: *"We must advance into France by the quickest and easiest route . . . speed of action is Germany's trump card, while Russia's strong suit is an inexhaustible supply of troops."*

With Jules Cambon he had a platonic conversation about the horrors of war, which neither gentleman was destined to experience in person. The Frenchman said: *"When the old generation dies to make place for a new one, which has not experienced the horrors of war and is eager for bat-*

tle—and that happens about once in every forty years—mankind is visited by a war. That is the way of the world." It is the same cynical way in which, in the old drawing-room comedies, the seducer used to say to the weeping girl: *"C'est la vie."*

The conversation between the German Chancellor and the British Ambassador the same evening is not so frank; in fact, there has seldom been so much lying on both sides as in this historical hour.

Bethmann, who had wanted to avoid war at all costs, and now saw too late how his weakness had entrapped him, said in moral indignation: *"This is like striking a man from behind while he is fighting for his life against two assailants!"*

Goschen: *"We are embarking on a life-and-death struggle for our honour, which we have solemnly pledged to defend Belgium's neutrality."*

Bethmann: *"But at what a price! Just for a word —neutrality, a word which in wartime has so often been disregarded; just for a scrap of paper, England is going to make war on a kindred nation who desires nothing better than to be friends with her. All my policy has tumbled down like a house of cards!"*

This *"scrap of paper"* was more genuine in its cynicism than the Englishman's phrases about his honour. Rather than speak openly of England's interests in Belgium, Goschen now becomes romantic: *"This,"* he says, *"is the dramatic climax of this tragedy. Our nations are falling apart just at the moment when the relations between them are more friendly and cordial than they had been for years."* It is only when he is going, and thus symbolising the breach between the two nations, that he finds the words which reveal the whole thing for a mere war of Cabinets: *"Unfortunately, notwithstanding our efforts to maintain peace between Russia and Austria, the war has spread and has brought us face to face with the situation which . . . we cannot possibly avoid. . . . This unfortunately entails our separation from our late fellow-workers. You will readily understand that no one regrets this more than I."*

To the tune of such general phrases of regret, covering the lack of genuine reasons, the Frenchman and the Englishman left Berlin.

* *

Count Berchtold, who had begun the game, was now disinclined to play it to the end. When he saw that all was over between Berlin and Petersburg, he felt that the desired opportunity had come for again choosing between two Cabinets. The pupil

of Metternich, faced with this alternative, does not
hesitate to decide for the Russian! On the last day
of July, when the breach between Germany and
Russia, brought about by Berchtold himself, finally
became a fact, in that very hour the Viennese Count
for the first time smiled again, as it were, across
the Neva and suddenly began the *"conversations"*—
those negotiations which Grey had tried vainly for
a week to bring about. Now for the first time Berlin saw the danger. *"We forgot,"* wrote Tirpitz,
*"to ask Austria whether she would fight with us
against Russia. To my horror Moltke said to me
that if the Austrians drew back we should be forced
to conclude peace at any price."*

Great is the joy of the enemy over this turn in
the Nibelung camp. They hope to separate Vienna
from Berlin at the last moment. On the first day,
when Germans and Russians are already shooting
at each other, Berchtold, that sudden convert to
peace, converses with the Russian Ambassador "in
friendly fashion" about Russia. The latter deplores Germany's lust for war and leaves him with
the shattering words: *"Indeed, there is nothing
between us except a great misunderstanding."*
Berchtold by his own admission finds no words in
favour of Germany, whom he has enticed into war,
either with the Russian Ambassador or afterwards

with his French colleague, whom, indeed, he allows
at this moment to make complaints about Kaiser
Wilhelm.

Meanwhile a rain of telegrams reaches Vienna
from Berlin, which now, with full justice, vigorously insists on the war which the others had concocted. The Austrian declaration of war on Russia really attempts, in its grotesquely complicated
official style, to give the impression that Vienna has
been forced into war by Berlin.

But why break with France? Why break with
England, so long united to Vienna by ties of culture and business? Thousands of German dead
already lie on the battlefields rotting for the greater
honour of the murdered Hapsburg; Count Berchtold, however, continues courteously to receive daily
visits from the enemies of his ally. It is a pity that
Frenchmen take their politics so seriously; they are
absolutely bent on breaking with Vienna, although
Vienna can see no reason for it! A week after
beginning war with Germany, the Frenchman asks
Vienna whether Austria has sent troops to Alsace.
Berchtold indignantly denies it. How can anyone suspect him of such conduct? The Germans,
however, who have every reason to be getting uneasy as to their allies joining at last in the war in
the West, now spread rumours in the neutral coun-

tries that they are fighting almost everywhere *"shoulder to shoulder with Austria."* Then old Monsieur Dumaine becomes more and more urgent in Vienna; once again he puts his question, receiving renewed reassurances. At last he curtly states that Austrian troops have been moved West, and that he requests his passports. Profound regret at the Ballplatz. Only the Burgomaster of Vienna thinks, "If these Frenchmen are determined to shoot at us, I'll give them a lesson"; and the same evening announces from the balcony of the Rathaus: *"Revolution in Paris! The President assassinated!"*

Meanwhile the British Ambassador also remains peacefully in Vienna, and the Austrian in London. When Prince Lichnowsky leaves London the Ambassador of his ally sees him off at the station, and complacently announces that he, for his part, hopes to be stopping on. And, indeed, he does stop nine days more; he is unable to send telegrams in code, but he has repeated conversations with Grey on some form of separate understanding.

"Would it not be better to avoid all hostilities between us?" asks Count Mensdorff. *"Would it not be desirable that two Powers, one from each group, should remain in contact with each other?"* When the press calls on him to be gone at last,

Grey, the enemy, says to him: *"I hope you do not feel insulted."* Lord Rosebery visits him at his Embassy, complains to this Austrian about his Russian allies, and prophesies that by playing this game England will only help the Tsar to rule over the world.

At the same time Count Berchtold receives imploring telegrams from Berlin: *"German ships of war in the Mediterranean need Austrian help against the English Fleet."* This estimable ally tries once more to avoid a direct answer, whereupon an ultimatum comes from Berlin: *"War against England must be declared within five days, on the 12th of August at the latest."*

"How infernally energetic these Prussians are!" thinks Berchtold, still hoping to find some way of wriggling out of the difficulty. But when the 12th draws near, the English, with their usual politeness, help the Viennese out of their difficulty; they send Count Mensdorff home.

Next morning—it is August 13th, and Germany, who has gone into the war as Austria's second, has been fighting for a fortnight with fearful losses— the British Ambassador calls on Berchtold who, *"with the courtesy which never leaves him, deplores the destiny"* which is sending two such good friends to the battlefield to fight each other. When they

run dry of ideas, diplomats are fond of falling
back on destiny.

Bunsen, *"with emotion in his voice,"* replies:
*"Nor do we see any reason, however distant, for a
conflict. May I beg Your Excellency to express to
His Majesty my profound gratitude for all the
marks of friendship and consideration which I have
received in the last eight months, and assure him
of the profound respect of His Majesty the King,
who regards His Majesty with deep veneration,
and expresses the hope that the most regrettable
state of war between Great Britain and the Monarchy may be of no long duration."*

Berchtold: *"I am extremely perturbed at the
thought that we find ourselves in conflict with England, as the two countries are so near to one another,
politically and morally, by traditional sympathies
and their common interests. Allow me to share
your hope that this most regrettable state of war
will be of no long duration, and that normal relations will soon be restored."*

Next day Austrian and English sailors were
shooting one another dead in the Mediterranean
under the flags of their respective rulers, who entertained such admiration for one another's persons. Millions were forced by their superiors to
hate one another from to-day onward, and the

majority actually believed that they did so;
throughout whole decades this hatred, concocted
by criminals, will live on in the children of these
fighters. Throughout four long years, every man
who sends a greeting to his son or his father on
the enemies' side will be gaoled as a traitor. But
the Emperors and Kings by the grace of God
assure one another, through their functionaries,
how deeply they regret the incident, and meanwhile wish one another Godspeed.

In days of old kings rode before their troops
of mercenaries, and decided the struggle in
nightly duel. To-day they force their peaceable
subjects first into hatred, then into the trenches,
but call it "chivalrous" not to bombard one another's headquarters, thus sparing among millions
only their equals; thus putting themselves in a
position to hope for early restoration of the normal relations which they have wantonly destroyed.

Two weeks later, when Brussels was already
under German administration, poor Austria had
no alternative left but, here also, to take the final
step. At last she declared war upon Belgium.

During the last interviews, tears were shed, according to the official reports, on five occasions.
King Carol of Roumania wept in the presence of

Count Czernin, the honest tears of a noble and
righteous ruler taken by surprise. Pashitch wept
comprehensible tears of joy in Nish in the presence
of the Russian Chargé d'Affaires. Goschen wept
before Bethmann when taking leave. Sazonov and
Pourtalès reproached one another with tears. As
all these tears appear only in the enemy's reports,
one must conclude that diplomats consider it un-
fitting to weep for the misfortunes of nations for
which they are responsible; it is better form to let
the common people weep. Only it is written otherwise in the Book of History.

*   *

Wavering hands have cast a stone from the
heights on which kings and ministers stand; already it is rolling, soon it pursues its downward
path with mad velocity—an avalanche. During
these first days all the Governments basked in the
sunshine of a victory whose full rays were never
to fall on any one of them. The masses have been
won over. Already the victims of treachery are
confidingly shouting and hating through the Capitals of Europe.

In Vienna the enthusiasm went to the familiar
waltz time. The masses were organised in gala
parades under the protection of the fire brigade;

the *Prince Eugene March* resounded in practised chorus along the Ring as far as the Rathaus, from whose balconies ladies in elegant summer toilets waved their handkerchiefs; all was beautiful, gay, and well-staged.

Here a focus was lacking: for the Emperor, living at Schönbrunn, hardly more than a myth, was seldom to be seen; no one knew the new heir to the throne by sight, and for decades past most of the Ministers had lived behind clouds which hid them from the vulgar gaze. Thus the people had to celebrate the great festival in its own fantastic way. On August 5th the two Allied Emperors were represented in tableaux vivants on a stage in this city of theatres. Vienna, the musical city, celebrated the outbreak of war in her garden restaurants with her own songs. It seemed a city of festival.

In Berlin ominous presentiments, if uttered aloud, were drowned in the general shouts. The serious temper of the masses, under the searchlight of nationalism, went up in amazing fireworks. The military spirit drilled into them gave the whole scene a march-rhythm which "made every Prussian heart beat higher." When heavy, grey lorries came along the Linden on the afternoon of August 1st, and young men, grey and dirty in their working-blouses, flung special editions of the papers into the streets, not singly, but in whole packets, the crowds joyously acclaimed them as though they were messengers of victory, and the rolls of papers, still moist, were passed from hand to hand.

In the evening tens of thousands marched to the Palace in the hope of seeing the Kaiser. He spoke from the balcony:

"*I know no parties now. I know only Germans.*" A splendid thought, incarnated as a winged word, and for the time being still endowed with authority, so that the crowd believed in it.

The Royal Palace gave Berlin that focus which was lacking in Vienna. The Princes driving in their cars along the street, Bethmann Hollweg, the Chancellor, who in a speech had the audacity to recall Bismarck—they were all smiles. Yes, it was all like a celebration of victory. The Kaiser alone carried an anxious face through the streets.

Berlin was in the power of the Generals. When Szögyény, at the last moment, tried to protest against the invasion of Belgium, the Foreign Office gave him this typically Prussian answer: "*The Military have the word now; no one can interfere.*" Moltke dictated the political telegrams to the Foreign Office, as suggested to him by his own subordinates. It was not the statesman in charge who decided what should be sent out. The ideas of some colonel or other became the high political voice of the realm.

The General Staff ordained: *"We wish to emphasise the fact that we are not taking possession of Belgian territory on some frivolous pretext. In this war it is a question for Germany not only of her whole national existence, but also of the preservation and maintenance of German civilisation and principles as against uncivilised Slavdom."*

A Note in this style was to be sent in clear to London *"as it will not do us any harm if this Note, by reason of its uncoded form, should become known also elsewhere."* This Note, slightly altered, was in fact sent in clear and in English to London as an instruction—to the detriment of Germany, for official arrogance was thereby for the first time revealed to the eyes of a hostile world, and was held to be the general sentiment of a nation which, as a whole, was as peaceable as its neighbours.

Next day the political vision of the General Staff embraced the whole earth. Moltke to Bethmann: *"An insurrection has been initiated in Poland. Already our troops are being greeted by the Poles almost like friends. . . . The feeling in America is friendly to Germany. American public opinion is indignant at the shameful manner in which we have been treated. .... It is of the greatest impor-tance to start insurrections in India and Egypt, also in the Caucasus. By means of the Treaty with Turkey the Foreign Office will be in a position to excite the fanaticism of Islam.*" No; this is no parody. It stands so in the Documents. The Sec-retary of State for Foreign Affairs had even wired to Constantinople the Mohammedan watch-word: "*It would be desirable to revolutionise the Caucasus.*"

Jagow vanished under the military forms, not only metaphorically. In shining groups they gather in the White Hall of the Palace; not round the throne, for that stood in lonely splendour be-tween the windows, but at a suitable distance. Among the tall generals in field-grey the German Secretary of State picked his hesitating steps from group to group, his narrow shoulders bowed, listen-ing, nodding, obviously seeking information every-where, whereas he should have been the centre to which inquiries were directed. Bismarck's spirit was not visible; it was only long afterwards that Ballin's pregnant remark was understood: "*A man need not have been a Bismarck to prevent this most idiotic of all wars.*" The Kaiser hurled his curses against the sinful world: "*The world is witness how unwearyingly we were in the first ranks of those who, in the stress and confusion of the last years, sought to spare the peoples of Europe a war between the Great Powers. . . . In self-defence, with clean consciences and clean hands we seize the sword.*" Doubtless he had long since forgotten that on the 5th of July he had promised Austria unconditional support in her adventure. Doubtless he felt his cause to be holy and just, and issued his appeal to the world in complete good faith. Such was his character.

That afternoon, two hours later, the Chancellor expounded to the Reichstag the origin of the conflict, omitting, however, all the decisive factors. He thought the best way to deal with the Belgian affair was to give an honest account of it. About this march through Belgium, which had been the basis of the German plans for twenty years, Bethmann said: "*We are now in a state of necessity, and necessity knows no law. . . . France could wait! . . . The wrong—I speak openly—the wrong we thereby commit we will try to make good as soon as our military aims have been attained. Who has been menaced as we are, and is fighting for his highest possession, can consider only how he is to hack his way through.*" It was the right tune—the Reichstag thundered with applause. All Germany adopted the new dogma. The Professors of

Law and the Church supported it. Professor Kohler proved as a jurist why necessity knows no law, and Pastor Traub wrote: *"The fact that the Chancellor admitted our wrong turned it into a right."* Only the extremists felt a cold shudder, divining that to-morrow this idea would split the world into two camps.

In a cold voice, like a man condemned to death, Haase, the German leader of the Socialists, voted for the war credits in the name of four million German workers. Every sentence of his speech condemned the war for which he was voting the money: " *. . . in closest agreement with our French brothers. We are thinking too of the mothers who must give their sons, of the women and the children. . . . We feel ourselves in harmony with the International, which has always recognised the right of every people to full independence, and we condemn every war of conquest. We demand that the war be brought to an immediate end when the object of security is attained, and when the enemy is ready to conclude peace."*

On the Right the Junkers wish the devil would fly away with this pack of Reds. Can't they drop their speechifying even to-day? But what happens? No more speakers were on the paper; yet a man with a strikingly stern face presses forward to the tribune. It is Karl Liebknecht. Even as his brave father fought for many years on this spot, with the courage of a solitary prophet who knows only the inward voice, so now he dares—one against sixty million! But the President shakes his long, grey beard and refuses to let this dangerous man speak. As all parties are agreed, Liebknecht, too, gives way and votes for the five thousand million marks. When a vote was taken on the next credits, six deputies voted against them; and on the next occasion after that, thirty-two.

*   *

In the same hour that Bethmann and the Kaiser were defending Germany before God and history as the victims of aggression, Viviani, the French Premier, was reading the following message from the President to four hundred deputies in the Palais Bourbon:

"France has just been the object of a violent and premeditated attack. . . . This attack, which nothing can excuse, has been committed without declaration of war. . . . Our frontier has been violated in more than fifteen places. Belgium and Luxemburg have been attacked. France has been unjustly challenged; she wanted no war. She made every effort to avert it. The liberties of Europe, which France and her Allies and friends

*are proud to feel themselves defending, are in
danger."*

One man in this great house is affected more
strongly than all the others. The applause leaves
him cold; his emotion is too deep. It is the Russian
with the Pasha's head. It is the man who said in
these days: *"This is my war!"* It is Isvolski, the
Russian Ambassador in Paris. He called that day
"the proudest day of my life," and said to the
Spanish Ambassador: *"Four years at my post
have been enough to reach my end."*

But it is only in Russia that they understand
how to stage such moments truly in the grand
manner. The afternoon before last, at the same
hour, the brilliant carriages drove over the Neva
and through the portals of the Winter Palace.
Five thousand men, the first in the land, were soon
thronging the gallery of St. George. Everything
was shining as for a great festival, and yet all were
silent. The Court dresses of the ladies shimmer;
their jewels glitter. Noiselessly the Court enters.
Near the altar in the middle of the hall, the beautiful Tsarina stands with trembling lips, her eyes on
the ground, though her head is proudly lifted.
Even the Tsar seems like something symbolic. For
a long time the priests chant their minor litanies.
The Tsar prays silently.

Then old Goremykin reads the Manifesto aloud, exactly as in Berlin and Paris: *"We are the victims of aggression."* Once again God is invoked as witness. Now the Tsar rises, lays his hand on the Bible, and slowly begins:

"Officers of my Guard here present, I greet in you my whole Army and give it my blessing. I solemnly swear that I will never make peace so long as one of the enemy is on the soil of the Fatherland."

Thus spake the ancestor of this Romanov one hundred years ago. Now the Tsar embraces the French Ambassador. From without come shouts from the streets. The Tsar steps on to the balcony.

Hundreds of thousands are assembled on each side of the river, with their holy symbols, their flags, their pictures of the Tsar. In this moment, when he seems to them as a God, a hundred thousand men sink like one man on their knees. Yes, this is the last Tsar of the world; men prostrate themselves before him even as a thousand years ago. He alone, exalted above the masses, seems the real ruler over body and soul of the millions, by the Grace of God.

And yet this was the same crowd which, led by a priest, had approached the same spot nine years earlier to beg for liberty from their Little Father, the Tsar. Then Cossacks fell on the masses with curved sabres and short carbines, riding down and shooting down all who refused to give way. And even to-day there are rebellious hearts among the kneelers. They sing the Tsar's hymn, but they feel that this is the last time. While still half be- lieving in his Godhead, some of these brains are already planning their revenge. Already Lenin was writing from his exile that Germany was no more guilty than her enemies.

The most astonishing scenes were those in Lon- don. For days at a time there was no happy face in the streets or the railway stations. Neither anger nor hatred was anywhere to be seen; only per- plexed countenances gazed at the green and red placards, extending the Bank Holiday to four days.

War! Thousands of pale, awed faces appeared near the Stock Exchange, for the incredible had happened. For the first time for decades the Stock Exchange was closed. In London the man in the street was less prepared and, therefore, more alarmed than anywhere on the Continent.

On August 4th things suddenly changed. When war was declared all seemed possessed by one thought. The Civil War in Ireland collapsed in a day. In vain the Socialist groups went on pouring out manifestoes and appeals. Within two days a million placards announced a hundred German atrocities. With all speed the suffragettes trimmed their sails to the wind. Germans, who had been welcome business-friends only yesterday, were now calumniated and assaulted.

The Nelson Monument rises into a blue summer sky. But a few days ago it had been the scene of a pacifist demonstration by the workers. What is the flood that surges to-day round that pillar, which four lions guard as though to scare the crowd away? Through the hot night troops of boys march in from the suburbs, then again citizens in groups and columns, marching from here to Whitehall and Parliament, and all shouting: "Down with the Kaiser and the Germans!"

Wild reports of events which never took place are spread by the hourly editions of the papers, and run from mouth to mouth. *Rule Britannia* resounds to the same stars which in this same hour are listening to *Deutschland, Deutschland über Alles, La Liberté! La France! God the All-Terrible!* and *Gott erhalte, Gott beschütze.* At the same hour the national songs are being sung in every capital of Europe, and beating hearts would fain assure themselves of God, of Justice, and the Guns.

Closer and closer the crowd throngs round the Nelson Column. Flags wave, but only of two kinds, for no Russian flag can be found at this moment in all England, the Embassy needing its own. Men now bestride the stone lions, pots of beer are reached up to them, endless cheers for England and the victorious war are raised, and concertinas and bagpipes accompany them.

Now a carriage rolls up with women in it. It halts. The men on the Monument pull the women out and up. They are Frenchwomen gaily dressed. Now they are dancing the can-can in the crowd to the strains of the concertina. It is the wedding-dance of the Entente. *Vive la France!* Long life to a country against whom England has fought for centuries! Ladies in elegant toilettes come out of the clubs and theatres with their escorts. Every carriage is stopped, cabs, cars, victorias. The ladies in them stand up, the gentlemen get out and fraternise with the crowd. From the carriages white necks gleam under their jewels. Bare arms wave to the dancers at the English hero's feet. For the next few weeks all Europe believes in a grotesque alliance of classes and castes.

*   *

Such was Europe on August 4th.

The lies and frivolity, the passion and fear of thirty diplomats, princes, and generals, for four years transformed peaceable millions into murderers and robbers, for purposes of state, leaving at the end the whole Continent a prey to barbarism, degeneracy, and poverty. Not one people made any lasting profit from it. All peoples lost what decades could not restore. A foreign continent was to hold us all in thrall to debt. Hate and bitterness was to poison the peoples which formerly vied with one another in peace.

Those who were guilty of all this remained unpunished and free. Of them all, only Suchomlinov suffered imprisonment. The two men who first wanted to avert the war, the Tsar and Count Tisza, were murdered by the people, the latter because he refused to flee; Count Stürgkh, who was not one of the chief war-mongers, was also slain. All other *personally responsible leaders of Europe* saved their lives by flight or because their people were indulgent; and yet not one of them had ventured to share the life at the front, except Tisza. Not one of all the names which signed Europe's declaration of war, directly or indirectly, will be found in a casualty list. The Grand Duke Nicholas and Isvolski; Berchtold, Bethmann and Kaiser Wilhelm; Yanushkyevitch and Moltke—they all live, or did live, on unmolested; all of them except Moltke outlasted the war. Not one of the conquered was brought before the Courts of his State. The murderer of the Archduke was tortured to death; the murderer of Jaurès was finally acquitted.

But the people of Europe paid the bill with nine million corpses.

DATE DUE